THEORIES OF AUTISM

THEORIES OF
AUTISM

Cheryl D. Seifert

Edited by Charlene Breedlove

UNIVERSITY
PRESS OF
AMERICA

Lanham • New York • London

Copyright © 1990 by
Cheryl D. Seifert

University Press of America®, Inc.
4720 Boston Way
Lanham, Maryland 20706

3 Henrietta Street
London WC2E 8LU England

Library of Congress Cataloging-in-Publication Data

Seifert, Cheryl D.
Theories of autism / Cheryl D. Seifert.
p.   cm.
Includes bibliographical references.
1. Autism.   I. Title.
[DNLM: 1. Autism.   WM203.5 S459t]
RJ506.A9S435   1990   616.89'82—dc20
DNLM/DLC for Library of Congress   89–70483 CIP

ISBN 0–8191–7718–0 (alk. paper)
ISBN 0–8191–7719–9 (pbk. : alk. paper)

∞ TM   The paper used in this publication meets the minimum requirements of
American National Standard for Information Sciences—Permanence
of Paper for Printed Library Materials, ANSI Z39.48–1984.

To Theodore C. Seifert, Jr.
and
Eleanore S. Seifert

Contents

1

Rethinking Theories of Autism

Most theories formulated to explain the mechanisms involved in autism have stemmed from the work of Bettelheim (1950, 1967). His concepts, drawn for the most part from notions of psychological causality, were widely accepted from the time of Kanner's original (1943) study to as recently as 1980.[1] Bettelheim regarded autism as a psychosis[2] and parents—in particular, the mothering person's rejecting, destructive intent during the golden age of infancy—as responsible for the child's intractable retreat from reality.

Bettelheim had witnessed that some prisoners in German concentration camps lacked any apparent reaction to the most cruel experiences. He paralleled this phenomenon with autism, interpreting the child's withdrawal as a denial of terrible emotional pain. In his mind, the child possessed near superhuman strength and by giving up speech after saying a few words was willfully defying his parents in a final effort of self-assertion (1967). From 1944 to 1973 Bettelheim (1974) worked at the Orthogenic School of the University of Chicago to create a therapeutic milieu that would foster reconstruction of the child's personality as he attempted to ascend from the emotional hell that presumably resulted from an insensitive and destructive environment.

The body of literature based on Bettelheim's theory speculated that "autism has essentially to do with everything that happens from birth on" (Bettelheim 1967, p. 393). The infant was thought to have normal biological intelligence, but refused to communicate as a defense against further harm. (The word *infant* is used to emphasize that most investigators thought the seeds of infantile autism were sown during infancy, not in childhood.)

These powerful speculations, founded on far-reaching psychoanalytic theory, have been gradually modified as our knowledge of
neurobiology has increased. According to Bender (1960, 1973), Chess
(1971, 1977), Goldstein (1959), Rutter (1978), and Wing (1970,
1979), autism is an abnormal biological condition, primarily affecting
intelligence functions. If the mechanism that results in autistic behavior is not a loss either of the ability or the willingness to communicate,
then one is led to wonder whether severe mental deficiency is the
trigger.

Bettelheim's concepts, based on the information of the day, may
reflect a lack of intensive and firsthand knowledge about infants. Bettelheim attributes to infants an extraordinary power to register subtle,
nonverbal cues and emotions, way beyond the capabilities of most
adults—almost beyond belief. Like other psychoanalytic theorists,
Bettelheim imbues the infant with too much prescience and too many
innate ideas, all within a consistent psychoanalytic framework that
attributes complex later experience to inarticulate early experience.

In an era when no one seemed to know what to do with autistic
children or took much interest in them, Bettelheim made a serious
attempt to help them and certainly drew attention to the problem. Now
it is time to move theory forward with the insights provided by new
information from the biological sciences. Rethinking does not stop,
and we must continue to question each new advance in the field. It may
be only human to resist change, but it is also necessary to break loose
from prior concepts, adding knowledge with the free and creative spirit
of scientific research.

In retrospect, however well-intentioned, Bettelheim's position was
no more than a hypothesis; to date, no research has established that
autism is a psychosis. Nor have the social and psychological characteristics of parents or families been proved to be associated with the
development of autism.

HUMAN-FIGURE DRAWING:
AN APPROACH TO AUTISM

Through art one can gain insight into the psychological world of the
autistic child. As discussed in Chapter 7, art serves the nonverbal autistic child as a ready means of communication.

When a child draws a person, he involves the whole of his perceptual, cognitive, and kinesthetic-motor development. Studies by

Goodenough (1926) and Koppitz (1968) have demonstrated that a child's mental stage can be measured and evaluated by systematic analysis of human-figure drawings. Their research, which concentrates on the psychological functions that underlie drawing, indicates that children eventually allow simplified schemes to appear as adequate representations of complex perceptions (see Chapter 4). Gradually, the children's personal perceptions, mental images, and affect[3] become increasingly complicated expressions in their drawings. Contemplation of these findings led to the investigation of how affect is expressed and controlled in the human-figure drawings of autistic children. (See *Case Studies in Autism: A Young Child and Two Adolescents* [Seifert 1990a] and *Holistic Interpretation of Autism: A Theoretical Framework* [Seifert 1990b] for a comparison of human-figure drawings in autistic children.)

2

Defining Autism

In 1943 Leo Kanner first described autism as a behavioral disorder in children. The June 1943 issue of the journal *Nervous Child* (now extinct) published a paper entitled "Autistic Disturbances of Affective Contact," which described aberrant behavior in 11 children (eight of them males), 2 to 8 years of age, brought to the Children's Clinic of the Johns Hopkins Hospital over a period of five years. The distinctive behavioral phenomenon of early infantile autism that was then recognized remained through four decades an enigma to researchers and to the families of those stricken with this heartbreaking childhood syndrome.

DEFINITION

Autism is defined (Bender 1960, 1973; Chess 1971, 1977; Goldstein 1959; Myklebust, Killen, and Bannochie 1972; Rutter 1978; Wing 1970, 1979) as a sign of central nervous system damage, in which withdrawal and affectlessness are secondary symptoms. A pattern of damage occurs in autism that is unusual within the brain-injured group itself—something has gone wrong in an atypical way.

While certain subgroups of children may have neuropathology, the mechanisms that account for the biological basis of the profound dysfunction in social and communicative development remain unknown. The vast majority of autistic children have such severe social and communicative pathology they score in the mentally retarded range on standardized tests throughout their lives. (Sixty percent of autistic children have measured IQs below 50; 20% between 50 and 70; and

20% score 70 or more [Rutter 1978; DeMyer, Hingtgen, and Jackson 1981].) Autism can exist in degrees, from mild to severe; IQ can be a measure of severity. The lower the IQ the more severe the symptoms, in some cases so severe as to be beyond hope. High-IQ autistics (IQ over 60 or 70) with communicative speech by the age of 5 learn more easily and behave more conventionally since they develop with age. The lower the IQ the more work is needed for improvement and the more the likelihood of deviant social responses such as smelling people, self-stimulation, and self-injury.

INCIDENCE

The incidence of children with autism determined by the statistically valued studies of Kanner (1969) and Rutter (1978) is about five in every 10,000; that is, one third as common as Down's syndrome. This estimate, considered "solid," is supported by studies conducted in Denmark, England, and the United States (Lotter 1966; Rutter 1967; Treffert 1970; Wing 1979). Similar studies describing the incidence of the conditions labeled *autisticlike* or *autistic and related communications-handicapped* suggest that these descriptions can be applied to approximately 15 out of 10,000 births. This would mean that at most there are approximately 300,000 people with autism and autistic conditions in the United States today, one third, or 100,000, between infancy and 21 years of age, and two thirds, or 200,000, who are 21 years of age and older. People with autism come from all classes of society and most live a normal life span.

GENERAL SYMPTOMATOLOGY

O'Gorman (1970, pp. 13–14) provides a descriptive six-point formulation of the features of the autistic syndrome.

1. Withdrawal from, or failure to become involved with, reality; in particular, failure to form normal relationships with people.
2. Serious intellectual retardation with islets of higher, nearly normal or exceptional intellectual function or skills.
3. Failure to acquire speech, or to maintain or improve on speech already learned, or to use what speech has been acquired for communication.
4. Abnormal response to one or more types of sensory stimulus (usually sound).

5. Gross and sustained exhibition of mannerisms or peculiarities of movement, including immobility and hyperkinesis, but excluding tics.
6. Pathological resistance to change. This may be shown by:
    a. Insistence on observing rituals either in the patient's own behavior or in those around him.
    b. Pathological attachment to the same surroundings, equipment, toys, and people (even though the relationship with the person involved may be purely mechanical and emotionally empty).
    c. Excessive preoccupation with particular objects or certain characteristics of them without regard to their accepted functions.
    d. Severe anger or terror or excitement, or increased withdrawal when the sameness of the environment is threatened (e.g., by strangers).

AN ETHOLOGICAL COMPARISON

The Tinbergen Approach: A Reconsideration

The important contribution of E. A. Tinbergen and N. Tinbergen[1] was to enlarge on the social aspects of a psychogenic model of infantile autism while yet accepting an organic influence. In a Nobel Prize-winning work, "Early Childhood Autism: An Ethological Approach" (1972), on the potential causes and nature of early infantile autism, E. A. Tinbergen and N. Tinbergen (1972) and N. Tinbergen (1974) applied ethological theory to the autistic syndrome, emphasizing its origins in social stress. In later work (1976, 1983) their theory incorporated possible organic influences. They contended that autism, as a stress disease, is on the increase in Western and Westernized countries, and that failure to develop social bonding either temporarily or permanently can occur as a result of the modern, urbanized, crowded, rationalized, and stressful environment acting on a child who is timid by nature.

S. J. Hutt and C. Hutt first observed that, on occasions when truly autistic children do make social contacts, their behavior is similar to that of normal children. They state that "apart from aversion of the face, all other components of the social encounters of these autistic children are those shown by normal nonautistic children" (Hutt and Hutt 1970, p. 147). Tinbergen and Tinbergen's papers lend support to this view, hypothesizing that the autistic state is characterized by an affective imbalance in which fear, anxiety, or apprehension dominate and suppress many forms of social and exploratory behavior. The ethological approach has three main aspects:

1. a more intensive use of nonexperimental observations of autistic children, both when studying their behavior and when planning their treatment;
2. a comparison of the behavior of autistic children with that of normal children; and
3. observation of the behavioral fluctuations of both autistic and normal children in relation to environmental changes. Ethological theory also contains constructive ideas about the nature of autism, its genesis and development, and treatment and prevention.

Theoretically, a continuum exists between normal and autistic children, based on observations that the behaviorally autistic bouts of normal but apprehensive children overlap considerably with the more behaviorally normal periods of autistic children. At times, normal children can show all the behavior typical of autistic children; conversely, if a young autistic child is left alone in his favorite surroundings, he can shed many of his peculiarities and behave in a surprisingly normal manner.

Normal Child–Stranger Encounters

Tinbergen and Tinbergen's (1972) experiments with child–stranger encounters testify that there are certain procedures in a meeting with normal children (mainly toddlers) that strongly influence their reactions. These procedures can induce in children, who initially respond to an adult with mild but definite components of Kanner's (1943) syndrome, a rapid change toward normal, often even intensive social behavior. What really happens in social encounters is apparently not entirely appreciated. Normal children's responses are extremely varied, ranging from the unmistakably positive (such as an uninhibited smile, or even an approach and friendly interaction) to rejection and outright fear, expressed in gaze aversion, closing eyes, turning the head and even the whole body, and snuggling against the mother, along with many subtle, intermediate response patterns. A normal child beginning eye contact (looking at a stranger, who looks at the child) can show friendly behavior, welcoming eyes and body stance, continued eye contact, and a beaming smile. In other instances, an exploratory glance can be followed by a mild expression of rejection and an empty, blank expression (Figs. 2-1 and 2-2). If the response of

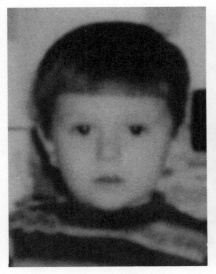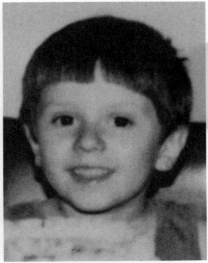

Figure 2-1. Two photographs of an autistic boy, age 5, taken in the same period: *left,* by a family friend; and *right,* by his father.

the adult to the child's behavior has a powerful communicative effect on the child, and if the observer keeps looking at the child and a few seconds later the child finds the adult still looking at him, the subsequent response can be either positive or negative.

Classification of Observations

Encounter-behavior can be categorized into socially positive and socially negative—bonding or sociable, and rejecting or withdrawing. Within each of the two classes, ''mild'' and ''strong'' provide a quantitative rating supplemented by qualitative distinctions; for example, closing the eyes might be rated as a ''milder'' negative response than turning away.

Complexity

While elaborating on the claim that normal children under certain circumstances show many (and not only visual) aspects of behavior usually found in autistic children, Tinbergen and Tinbergen (1972) found cases of normal children who show the same mixed response patterns (viz., withdrawal on the one hand and hyperkinesis on the other—observed in a 2½-year-old child recovering from surgery in a

Figure 2-2. Two photographs of a moderately autistic child taken by his father. *Left,* age 3 years, 3 months, shows withdrawal from an outer world of people into an inner world of things. *Right,* age 3 years, 6 months, with his mother—holding his knees together. Body language shows distrust. His appearance gives reason for worry and concern.

hospital). In normal children clumsiness may be combined with perfect motor control in some areas, and perceptual dysfunction combined with striking perceptual acuity, but mixed response patterns are more typical of autistic children. It appears, therefore, that (1) otherwise normal but relatively timid children can, in situations that carry unfamiliar social or physical elements, be made temporarily autistic and show all the symptoms of permanently autistic children; (2) there are gradations between normal and autistic children; and (3) the early social environment can play a part in promoting autism.

Motivational Conflicts

Tinbergen and Tinbergen introduced the important concept of motivational conflicts on the nonverbal level, which they applied to autistic children, studying them by ethological methods. N. Tinbergen's (1959, 1964) well-known experiments on the process of bonding and socialization in herring gulls and black-headed gulls led to an ingenious approach in the study of human autism (Tinbergen and Tinbergen 1972). N. Tinbergen's work on the courting patterns of gulls was applied to the observation of three autistic children and "many" (numbers unstated) young normal children.

Tinbergen and Tinbergen (1972) indicate that the encounter between a child and a strange adult creates a motivational conflict in the child, similar to that of female gulls in the pair-formation state, except that the approach tendency in children is not sexually motivated. The child shows attracted behavior to the stranger, yet definitely afraid behavior (timid, shy, anxious, insecure, etc.), indicating a motivational conflict and an emotional imbalance in which the child's fear or apprehension dominate, suppressing his social and exploratory behavior. For example, passing attacks of autistic behavior may appear in a normal child when he finds himself in a situation that creates a conflict between two incompatible motivations. On the one hand, the situation may evoke fear and a tendency to withdraw physically and mentally; on the other, it may elicit social and exploratory behavior that fear inhibits the child from pursuing. Children who are timid (by nature, nurture, or both), according to Tinbergen and Tinbergen, show this conflict behavior more readily than more resilient and confident children; however, all children respond to the environment in these terms.

Application to Children

An avoidance tendency can be recognized as (1) withdrawal from or defense against unfamiliar situations, (2) incomplete, inhibited attempts at socializing or exploration, (3) conflict movements, or (4) a mixture of the three. It is important to notice when children are *locking out, filtering out,* and *refusing to admit,* according to the particular sensory modality. Some primarily avoid visual input; some also reject auditory or tactile input. It is of utmost importance to realize that the relevant inputs are specific—that is, they specifically stimulate or reduce either the withdrawal system or the approach system. A child can actively develop and extend a capacity for this cutoff behavior. Cutoff is nonverbal and refers to any act or posture that occurs in a social situation for the express purpose of limiting social input.

This viewpoint moves the old problems of perceptual malfunctioning, quantity of input, and general arousal into a new light. There is no need, according to Tinbergen and Tinbergen, to seek the solution for autism in specific perceptual dysfunction, since the term inaccurately describes autistic behavior. Thus, the child who seems deaf (who, for

example, ignores acoustic social input) becomes intelligible. (Deaf-
ness is a common initial diagnosis for autistic children.)

The motivational conflict of timidity and fear on the one hand, and
approach and friendliness on the other, is solved in normal children
and those who are temporarily autistic if the stranger avoids stimulat-
ing withdrawal and positively elicits approach and contact. Accepting
that there are moment-to-moment fluctuations in the child's state because of the external situation and perhaps internal changes, the adult
must make continual adjustments. As with the gulls in N. Tinbergen's
(1959, 1964) experiment, very slight variations in the behavior of the
intimidating partner (the adult) influence the state of the timid partner
(the child): a straight look at a timid child, even when one is smiling,
could increase timidity in a temporarily or permanently cowed child.

The child's momentary state determines whether he will approach
or withdraw, and a child may on different occasions respond quite
differently to the same behavior of the same adult, depending on
whether the child feels secure or anxious. Thus we see a simple matter
of fluctuating thresholds, but the total social process seems so extremely variable because the standard by which the child responds is
also continually fluctuating, and these quick fluctuations in the child's
state are influenced by still other external and perhaps internal changes
as well.

A method of continuously monitoring the subject and adjusting
experiments accordingly is vital. This method is appropriately applied
in Tinbergen and Tinbergen's (1972) experiments, where the state of
the child is used as the yardstick for standardization, rather than the
objectively, physically measured environment. The child is the relevant standard, but since that standard is changing all the time, the
child's behavioral reactions in social encounters have to be gauged
from second to second, so that the adult can adjust his behavior and not
exceed the threshold of withdrawal.

Experimental Testing

Tinbergen and Tinbergen (1972) infer that application of this procedure invariably leads quickly to establishing a social bond. If these
methods are applied in an initial meeting with a distrustful child, the
child will be put at ease and attracted. The success of the step-by-step
experimental procedure depends on the observer-cum-interferer recognizing that looking at a child has a potentially intimidating effect, even
when one is smiling and definitely when one makes more friendly,

motivated movements, such as approaching and generally crashing through the child's barrier. One also has the task of adjusting one's signal behavior each moment to any sign of conflict in the child, and in such a manner that one avoids increasing the withdrawal tendency, so that approach behavior will be interpreted by the child as nonintimidating and positively friendly. It should be remembered that specific behavior has been employed to prevent the child from withdrawing, and equally specific behavior to entice him into seeking contact. For example, it is not advised that a stranger stare into a child's eyes late in the first year, when normal children begin to fear strangers; that would ensure a fright response. Laughing with him, however, is good, and advised—at any age; laughing together at something or someone is one of the strongest bonding behaviors.

Taming a child is in some ways comparable to male gulls trying to win the confidence of a female (Tinbergen and Tinbergen 1972). Similarly, humans, subtly tuned, can "play" a timid child based on what he can tolerate.

The Tinbergens make clear the many differences among children: their level of dominance or timidity, their speed of bonding, and their aversion, all of which must be quickly assessed. Some children object to being touched, others to being spoken to, and others (the majority) to certain visual signs. The approach-withdrawal conflict is present up to an advanced stage of the bonding process and is far weaker in the young infant than in older infants who develop 8-months' anxiety. Tinbergen and Tinbergen believe it necessary that all of these considerations be quickly assessed for successful bonding to occur.

Care giving and the early environment are extremely important to those suffering from autism, because in the mother–child dyad the mother herself can behave overintrusively toward a child or even solicit overintrusive behavior from visitors. Deviations in behavior, with gradations between normal and autistic, may therefore be largely induced by the environment and may be due in part to damage to specific behavioral systems we call (1) timidity or fear, and (2) sociability. A combination of genetic and environmental factors, hypothetically speaking, produces an overly timid child, and encounters with adults would naturally take longer to swing toward bonding. In extreme cases, the oversensitivity produced by fearfulness may prevent the motivational conflict from being solved. Thus, the child enters into a vicious circle in which overactivating fear becomes progressive. The resulting lowered thresholds lead to fear responses vis-à-vis a greatly widened range of stimuli and can include signals that normally have a bonding effect, such as the adult face and a friendly smile. Particularly in a world crowded with strangers, continuously increased input into a child's fear system can starve the bonding process, even in normal children.

Causation, Prevention, and Treatment

In the Tinbergens' view, a core problem in autism is affective and social. We see it in the child's desperate, frustrated attempts at socialization, combined with constant and intense fear. It follows that some cases of autism may result more from early environmental influences than we generally assume. Said another way, the autistic child may not be a problem child but a victim of our stressful environment, so different from a primitive hunting and gathering society. In such a problem environment, even healthy, normal parental behavior may misfire. What, then, do Tinbergen and Tinbergen suggest as a means of educating the autistic child? They advise that we concentrate on avoiding intimidation and refrain from too much socially intrusive teaching in situations where this has a favorable result. They warn of the harmfulness of some procedures considered symptom treatments, for example, intrusive speech therapy, frightening conditioning procedures, and electric shock treatment. Some therapeutic procedures advocate focusing on the delicate problem of eye contact to the point of forcing direct eye-to-eye contact on a child. The Tinbergens caution that, if the interpretation of autism as a hypertrophy of fear or timidity is even in part correct, violent stimulation of an already oversensitive fright system might be the worst treatment.

The consequence of such forced treatment is increased tension that probably aggravates autism and gives rise to bizarre behavior. Even in normal children, withdrawal behavior, defensive behavior, or conflict movements could result. Excessive distance-keeping, hugging the wall, spinning, walking on tiptoe, gaze aversion or a bland eye expression, acoustic cutoff, hunched shoulders, stereotypes with obsessive routines and rituals, panic tantrums in response to social or physical intrusion, and overall muscular tension can be recognized as exaggerated and often rigidified forms of the behavioral categories mentioned above. (See *The Use of Self* [Alexander 1932].)

Treating the motivational disturbance, whether an expression of nature, nurture, or interactional theory, might well be the most effective therapy for the autistic child. The methods the Tinbergens (1972) view as best fulfilling the criterion for anxiety reduction and restarting spontaneous socialization and exploration are (1) treating the mother–child dyad and also the family to restore the initially defective affiliation with the mother by provoking increased maternally protective behavior, and (2) using operant conditioning to hasten the child's response to changes in the mother and to elicit a mutual emotional bond between mother and child, while refraining from the piecemeal teaching of particular skills. (See Clancy and McBride 1969; Kramer, Anderson, and Westman 1984 for two examples of treatments.) The primary treatment objective is to attack the predisposing factor of autism, interrupt the autistic process, and promote the mother–child bond. Not the child alone, but the family system of relationships is the real unit of treatment.

In summary, Tinbergen and Tinbergen's methodological approach to autism provides a wealth of careful, minute, and thorough observations of young children's behavior during a period of affect development. An act of intellectual intuition is required, however, to bring their approach into relationship with other research studies.

Tinbergen and Tinbergen's research has been criticized (Schopler 1974; Wing and Ricks 1976) for the imprecision with which the term *autism* is used, and for generalizing from a small number of cases (numbers unstated). The extended study presented in *Case Studies in Autism: A Young Child and Two Adolescents* (Seifert 1990a) lends support to the Tinbergens' view and treatment.

The taming procedure, defined by Tinbergen and Tinbergen with great precision, seems particularly effective in furthering progress in treating autism and problems of affect. These methodological principles and views enable us to revise the concept of the autistic child and direct our attention to the abundance of observations available to us.

The use of psychotherapeutic techniques and acceptance of an organic etiology distinguishes Tinbergen and Tinbergen's theory of autism from purely organic theory, which at present fosters little hope for prevention or treatment. If we ascribe at least some cases of autism to a problem of expression and control of affect, or to the interaction of a predisposing, possibly even temporary, organic factor and environmental influences that initiate the autistic process (i.e., the predisposing factor shapes the responses of the mother sufficiently for the autistic process to become stable and self-perpetuating very early in life), then the prospect for successful treatment is brighter.

This ethological approach to autistic behavior brings us closer to understanding autism by casting into sharper relief different aspects of the interrelationships between biological and environmental influences.

It has been possible to present here only the main course of thought dominating Tinbergen and Tinbergen's theory. The various interplays and meanings of this ethological approach and their methodological framework are well described in their paper. Their approach to autism shows the potential role of intimate interactions between biological and environmental factors and stimulates a better understanding and treatment of this set of behavioral aberrations.

3

An Evolutionary View
of Personality Development

Most current conceptions of psychodynamics and psychopathology originated with the work of Freud. By 1897, Freud had articulated the groundwork of psychoanalytic theory, which concentrated on the inner world of the individual psyche. Mendelian inheritance, first presented in 1865, was rediscovered by DeVries, Correns, and Tschermak in 1900, and led to the description of populations in mathematical terms.

Freud advanced his libido theory in the face of modern biology and made creative efforts to translate systematically psychological processes into physiological terms. The language of physiology set forth early on all but disappeared in Freud's later thinking, and his complex theoretical system remained only vaguely linked to the great advances in biology.

After 1900, there seemed to be few bridges left connecting psychoanalytic theory and modern biology. Freedman (Freedman, Loring, and Martin 1967), a contemporary sociobiologist, has shown how Darwin's general theory of evolution provides such a broad conceptual base as to readily incorporate the facts of an interpersonal psychology. This does not preclude psychodynamic thinking, since modern biological thinking acknowledges the importance of environment and genotype in the basic genetic formula: genotype $\times$ environment $=$ phenotype, and since genotype implies phylogeny, it provides a basis for a wider range of thought than any existing psychological theory (Freedman, Loring, and Martin 1967). Tensions in the field of psychology are expressed and reconciled in Freedman's combined evolutionary and holistic "approach from above,"[1] perhaps the best hope for reconciling the psychoanalysis of Freud with the modern biology of neo-Darwinists.

17

FREEDMAN'S BIOLOGICAL APPROACH

Freedman's evolutionary view of man deals specifically with genetics and human evolution (1958, 1961, 1963, 1964, 1965a, 1965b, 1967, 1968a, 1968b, 1971a, 1971b, 1971c, 1971d, 1974, 1975a, 1975b, 1976, 1979; Brazelton and Freedman 1971; Freedman and Freedman 1969; Freedman and Keller 1963; Freedman, King, and Elliot 1961; Freedman, Loring, and Martin 1967; Freedman and Omark 1973). He and co-workers focus on the evolution and development of behavior and how behavioral patterns have evolved by means of innate genetic factors interacting with environments.

Personality is defined as "a Gestalt array of species traits, usually related to interpersonal behavior, which varies uniquely for each individual because the genotype is unique, the individual experience is unique, and the interaction between genotype and experience is unique" (Freedman, Loring, and Martin 1967, p. 470). Freedman (1971a) suggests that behavioral traits such as social attachment, fear, autonomy, imitation, curiosity, verbal communication, sex differences in aggression and passivity, and other essential behaviors are evolutionary developments and species-specific. Bowlby (1958) studied the nature of the child's tie to his mother and proposed an evolutionary view of attachment formation. Bowlby's thesis is that the child's first object relations form the foundation of his personality. Freedman's (1971a) reply rebuts Bowlby's thesis:

> The point is that early attachments *are* personality and that we are persons, or personalities, from the very start. To speak of these early attachments as causing personality is to commit the logical fallacy of *tabula rasa* mind—where there was nothing, something eventually appears. While it is true one is always becoming, one is also always *being*, and the style in which these early interactions occur is itself personality. Each infant negotiates these behaviors in a unique way, that is, in his very own variation of the basic species' theme. (p. 260)

Freedman's biological approach does not deny that environment influences behavior and personality; it does deny its causal status.

Individual Differences

The basis for evolution is variation and mutation of genetic material, which provides individuals with the diversity necessary to respond differently and more or less successfully to environmental pressures. Until the middle of the 19th century, one of the major obstacles in the way of a scientific appreciation of organic evolution was the widely accepted notion of fixed species, which pictured all living forms as static entities, unchanged in the past and unchangeable in the future. A species was thought of as a morphological "type," distinct from the morphological types of other species; therefore no species could have arisen from another—a notion promulgated by philosophers, religious institutions, and many biologists. Such typological descriptions were valuable in separating one group of organisms from another, but of far greater importance was the fact that members of a species departed, in differing degrees, from the idealized types.

Darwin's attempts to understand biological change in support of evolution led him to discard the doctrine of fixed species. He argued that, although there were morphological species types, they arose by natural selection among the variable members, and the boundaries between species were truly changeable and fluid. The tendency for populations to increase by reproduction, combined with the fact that most populations were stationary in size, led to the condition called the struggle for existence. This struggle implies that death by any means can prevent all offspring of a species from surviving to reproductive age.

Considering all the possible variations carried by most species, the struggle for existence led to the selection and proliferation of only those organisms well adapted to their environment and most successful in mating. "Survival of the fittest" is a term originally laden with moral connotations, but in modern biological terms "fittest" means no more than having the most reproductive success in a particular environment, whether such success is achieved by strength or weakness. Darwin used these concepts to point out that, as the environment changes, fitness changes, and evolution continues to proceed.

Dobzhansky and Spassky (Dobzhansky 1937) demonstrated evolution in laboratory experiments by intentionally disturbing the harmony between an artificial environment and the fruit flies living in it. At first the environmental change killed most of the flies, but during consecutive generations most strains showed a gradual improvement in viability, evidently owing to the environment's selection of the better-adapted variants.

In a discussion of individual personality differences, Freedman, Loring, and Martin (1967) remind us of many forms of typology in personality theories, for instance, the systems of Jung (extraversion-introversion) Kretschmer (cyclothymic-schizothymic), Sheldon (endomorphy-mesomorphy-ectomorphy), and Freud (oral-anal-phallic). They cite the following:

> The typological concept has been completely displaced in evolutionary biology by the population concept. The basis of this concept is the fact that in sexually reproducing species no two individuals are genetically alike, and that every population is therefore to be characterized only by statistical parameters such as means, variances, and frequencies. . . . Genetic variability is universal, a fact which is significant not only for the student of morphology but also for the student of behavior. It is not only wrong to speak of *the* monkey but even of *the* rhesus monkey. The variability of behavior is evident in the study not only of such a genetically plastic species as man but even of forms with very rigid, stereotyped behaviors such as the hunting wasps. . . . The time has come to stress the existence of genetic differences in behavior, in view of the enormous amount of material the students of various forms of learning have accumulated on nongenetic variation in behavior. (Mayr 1958, pp. 352–53)

In other words, assuming that personality has biological roots, any search for a stable typology of personality is all too simplistic and "a doomed project before it starts" (Freedman, Loring, and Martin 1967, p. 472).

In sexual reproduction, gametes carry a mixture of parental chromosomal material (in diploid populations, two sets of chromosomes, one set paternal and one set maternal). A pool of chromosomal material is, in essence, created in the sex organs of an individual through the contributions of both parents from which, in turn, the reproductive cells may draw various combinations. A species can consist of so many individuals acting as parents that each generation represents a reshuffling of chromosomal material on a very large scale. The advantage this chromosomal variability offers—one unobtainable in asexual reproduction and the reason for sexual reproduction being such a widespread phenomenon—is that the greater the variability of a species, the greater number of changes it will survive in time. The biological and environmental factors on which the success of an organism depends are not typically constant from place to place or time to time. Therefore, if changes in chromosomal material result in changed biological characteristics, a greater variety of chromosomal material will lead to an increased probability of a species surviving under the varied conditions in which it must live. Said another way, most living organisms take advantage, at some time in their life cycles, of the opportunity to exchange and reshuffle their genetic material. Said yet another way, "Natural selection is a mechanism for generating an exceedingly high degree of improbability" (Huxley 1943, p. 474).

The number of genes in a single organism is not known with 100% precision; however, it has been estimated to be in the thousands, at least in the higher organisms. *Drosophila* has been estimated to have 5,000 to 12,000 genes; for man the figure is probably higher. Assuming the human species has only 1,000 genes and that each gene has only two variants, even on this conservative basis, Mendelian segregation and recombination would be capable of producing $2^{1,000}$ different genetic combinations in human beings. The combining power of the sexual process is astounding. On a conservative estimate, the number of possible gene combinations in the human species alone is far greater than that of the electrons and protons in the universe. That is, except in the case of identical twins, no two persons now living, dead, or to live in the future are at all likely to carry the same complement of genes. The mechanism of sexual reproduction, of which the recombination of genes is a part, forever creates new genetic constitutions on a prodigious scale, without ever encountering environmental variation. But environmental variation on the fine scale is just as subtly various as the individuals creating it.

Continuity Versus Discontinuity in Personality

To illustrate the environmental interaction over time of a carefully arranged genotype, animal studies with inbred groups have proved the most accurate and repeatable (Freedman, Loring, and Martin 1967). Freedman (1958) reared puppies of four dog breeds, either permissively or under strict training. At the end of rearing, he found that

> (1) Each breed (genotype) reacted to the same mode of rearing in a unique way. (2) The breed × environmental interactions varied kaleidoscopically, depending on the test or task imposed. (3) The same behavior in one breed might be due *primarily* to constitution and in another breed primarily to conditions of rearing (termed a "phenocopy" by geneticists). (4) In the followup period, which lasted over a year, three breeds showed a straight-line continuity in their social reactions to humans that was modeled on behavior learned during early rearing. (5) In one breed the permissively reared animals changed markedly over time, whereas the disciplined group continued to show the same fawning behavior developed in puppyhood. (6) Some breeds were more deeply affected by the early modes of rearing than others. (Freedman, Loring, and Martin 1967, p. 476)

Freedman, Loring, and Martin (1967) contend that an ethological study such as this one (1958) offers a reasonable, general paradigm for analogous genotype and environmental interactions occurring in hominid growth.

In human behavioral genetics, twins provide some of the most convincing data for determining the proportion of variation in a trait due to differences in environment or differences in heredity. Identical twins have identical genes since all the cells of each twin are descendants of the same fertilized egg. Fraternal twins result from the simultaneous production of two eggs by the female. They are separately fertilized by different sperms and each develops into a different embryo. Such twins grow in separate embryonic membranes and are genetically no more similar than two siblings (with the genetic correlation between dizygotic co-twins estimated to be .50). The total frequency of twins varies in different population groups; in the United States, identical twins appear only one third as frequently as fraternal twins.

Identical twins are alike in genotype; therefore, differences between members of a pair result from the environment. Fraternal twins share the same environments and differences due to their genotypes. The extent to which fraternal twins differ more than identical twins is a measure of hereditary factors.

To assess the degree to which genetic factors determine behavior, Freedman (1963, 1965a) studied mental and motor abilities and personality development in 20 pairs (11 fraternal pairs and nine identical pairs) of same-sexed infant twins. He chose to study infant twins because imitation, which is independent of immediate perception, starts after the first year. Thus the factor of mutual contagion could be ruled out. By studying infant twins he was able to postpone zygosity determinations until after the study and he also avoided the unreliability of retrospective histories.

All infants in Freedman's (1963) study were filmed, and a coworker independently studied the infants. Freedman found that identical twins show greater concordance than fraternal twins in two areas of behavior: (1) development of positive social orientation, including smiling, and (2) fear of strangers. The greater concordance for personality development within identical pairs was considered a reflection of their hereditary similarity. Behavioral geneticists agree that all aspects of human behavior, abilities, talents, temperament, personality, and pathology contain genetic components (Erlenmeyer-Kimling and Jarvik 1963; Gottesman and Shields 1967; Vandenberg 1966). Freedman's (1963) study supports the data gathered from personality research on older twins (Freedman 1965a; Vandenberg 1966); that is, identical twins are more concordant for discrete traits. Freedman, Loring, and Martin (1967) assert there can be no reasonable doubt that genes mediate variations in intelligence and personality.

Yet no trait is absolutely fixed, for phenotype will change as does the interaction between heredity and environment (Freedman 1971a). This means there always will remain the possibility that some untried environment will extract new phenotypic changes from the genotype being studied. One major study by Newman, Freeman, and Holzinger (1937) of identical twins reared apart showed that both genetic and environmental components are involved in intelligence scores and in numerous other traits, but their relationship is not always constant.

Vandenberg (1966) speaks of relative fixity in a hierarchical arrangement of certain aspects of human behavior, using strength of F ratios as a reading. At the stable end of Vandenberg's hierarchy are primary mental abilities, then motor and perceptual abilities (measured by cognitive and sensory tests); at the labile end is personality (measured by personality tests).

At first glance, Vandenberg's data seem to indicate that some aspects of behavior are under greater genetic control than others, for example, performance on intelligence quotient tests versus performance on personality tests (Freedman 1971a). However, in a close analysis of Vandenberg's (1966) data, Freedman (1971a) applied the concept of homeostasis. Within this concept, behavior ranges from fixed, nonhomeostatic activities, such as reflexes, through behavior that is intentional and conscious and reflects a degree of abstract thought (Goldstein 1939). Abstract thought, as opposed to concrete thinking, is the ability to go beyond presentational constructions of here-and-now experience to an interpretative representation of present activities as well as past and future possibilities. From the evolutionary point of view, man is completely alone in his capacity to examine all his options in advance, to look inward, and to observe the processes of his own mind—in short, to think. Of even more importance, when man thinks, he knows he is thinking. Man's conscious thinking is one sign of species superiority that provides uniquely flexible adaptations.[2]

Vandenberg's fixity rating is best interpreted as a hierarchy of the amount of intentionality built into various facets of the human system (Freedman 1971a). In other words, "The ability to manipulate symbols in the abstract necessarily lowers concordance rates between identical twins, and it has its greatest effects in items associated with personality traits rather than in items associated with intelligence tests because personality items involve many more choice points'' (p. 234).

Freedman (1971a) cites Troup (1938) in pointing out that verbal responses to Rorschach ([1921] 1969) ink blots by identical twins are rarely similar. Each twin uses imagination, inventiveness, originality, creativity, and playfulness, resulting in unpredictable behavior. In comparison, intelligence tests require clearly right or wrong answers; choice is limited, and originality or creativity is not necessary. In other words, despite Vandenberg's data, primary abilities may be under no greater genetic control than personality when we can hierarchize the level of intentionality (leading to more predictability) and the use of abstract manipulation (leading to unpredictability) within the various sets of tasks (Freedman 1971a).

GENES AND AUTISM

In *The Comedy of Errors*, Shakespeare makes use of a device close to the hearts of Greek and Roman playwrights: he brings on stage identical twins. He describes them thus: ''The one so like the other, as could not be distinguish'd but by names.'' To add to the confusion, he gives each twin the same name. Moreover, each twin has a servant, and they too are identical twins with the same name. It is no wonder that errors arise.

Biology seldom imitates art so closely, however. Twins are relatively rare, particularly identical pairs, who represent only 0.3% of all births. Those who have had the benefit of closely observing identical twins are usually struck by their remarkable similarity. We know identical twins have identical sets of genes, represented by identical sequences of the paired nucleotides of DNA, thus providing tangible and simple proof of the power of inheritance. When, in contrast, we look at two people selected at random, enough differences are apparent that any likelihood of confusing them is remote. Individuality is a familiar property of humans; it marks not only facial features and bodily traits but even such details as fingerprints and voice. Conceivably, not even identical twins are wholly identical in every respect; it is only that the differences between them are almost always smaller than those between unrelated individuals.

Twin studies suggest that autism may be genetically linked to other cognitive disorders (Folstein and Rutter 1977a) caused by pathogenic genes. Ritvo, Spence, Freeman, Mason-Brothers, and Marazita (1985) found evidence compatible with autosomal recessive inheritance, e.g., autism expressed only in persons who received the recessive gene from both parents, and in families with multiple incidences of autism—autosomal recessive inheritance predicts 100% concordance in identical twins (both members of a twin pair exhibit a certain trait) and 25% concordance in fraternal twins.

In 1980, Ritvo, Freeman, and co-workers (Ritvo 1981) started a registry at the University of California at Los Angeles of families with autistic children. Freeman at first hoped they might find 25 multiple-incidence families to work with, but such cases were extremely difficult to locate. As of March 1985, 610 families were registered as having autistic members according to the 1980 American Psychiatric Association criteria. Analysis of these 610 families shows a surprisingly strong genetic factor in autism (Ritvo 1985).

For example, there are 23 pairs of identical twins; in 22 of these, both twins are autistic. By comparison, in only four of 17 pairs of fraternal twins are both twins autistic (Ritvo, Freeman, Mason-Brothers, Mo, and Ritvo 1985; Ritvo, Spence, Freeman, Mason-Brothers, and Marazita 1985). The odds of that happening by chance are very small. In 535 nontwin families there are 90 who have two autistic siblings, in eight there are three autistic children, and in 100 families autism is present in a second-degree relative (cousin, aunt, or uncle). Interestingly, 170 registered families have one autistic child plus another child with a developmental disability, such as retardation, schizophrenia, Down's syndrome, hyperactivity, or speech delay, and 167 families have one autistic child and a second-degree relative who is developmentally disabled. Again and again families are found with clusters of affected members. In an astounding case of two pairs of identical twins reported by Ritvo (1985), all four twins are autistic.

The premise examined here is that autism can be best explained by applying biological principles to individual behavior, thus reversing the focus from individual to evolutionary thinking.

Results from the study presented in *Case Studies in Autism: A Young Child and Two Adolescents* (Seifert 1990a) agree with Ritvo's (1981) assertion that heredity may play a role in autism as evidenced by the higher concordance in identical than in fraternal twins. The psychological method of the Seifert study complements Ritvo's study of twins and furthers our understanding of autism.

Potential genetic factors would account for the reported identical twin concordances (Folstein and Rutter 1977b) and the identical twin concordance rate of 95.7% in one major study (Ritvo, Freeman, Mason-Brothers, Mo, and Ritvo 1985). As we confirm that heredity too plays a role in autism, we are left with the question, "How does the environment interact with the genotype?"

The dramatic discovery by Courchesne and his co-workers (Courchesne et al. 1988) indicates again the importance of a genetic contribution to autism. Magnetic resonance imaging performed on 18 autistic people revealed measured hypoplasia (underdevelopment) of the vermal neocerebellum region of the brain. E. Courchesne (pers. com. November 1988) suggests, in a study in progress, the possibility of hypoplasia of the hemispheres. The finding makes it clear that at least in a substantial subset of autism, there is definite anatomical irregularity.

Because underdeveloped areas of the cerebellum form at different times and have a different developmental course than the nonaffected regions, Courchesne's research is an important first step in determining the timing of environmental or genetic mediated events that damage the brain and induce the autism disorder and in identifying other neural structures that may be concomitantly damaged.

Although we do not know what percent of autistic individuals would have clinical abnormalities, E. Courchesne (pers. com. November 1988) estimates that up to 20% appear to have gross abnormality of the cerebellum, 30% to 40% have mild abnormality, and others measure normal.

Interplay of Environmental Factors

Parents of autistic children have historically been portrayed in scientific literature as cold, aloof, and unstimulating to their children. Kanner (1949) described them as obsessive, perfectionistic, humorless individuals who use set rules as substitutes for life's enjoyments. Severe early stress to infants, such as parental rejection, separation, or maternal depression, have also been linked to autism (Bettelheim 1967).

Cox et al. (1975) compared early stress events and the warmth, responsiveness, and sociability of parents of autistic children who show normal nonverbal intelligence and no evidence of neurological disorders with parents of matched dysphasic children—those suffering language disorders due to injury or disease. The parents' groups did not differ in incidence of psychiatric conditions, housing, illness, finances, or interpersonal relationships. Ratings of emotional warmth and sociability were similar except that parents of autistic children spent more time with friends. Thus, parents of autistic children were as sociable, demonstrative, and emotionally responsive as the parents of dysphasic children.

McAdoo and DeMyer (1978a) compared the Minnesota Multiphasic Personality Inventories (MMPIs, Hathaway and McKinley 1943-67) of parents of autistic children with a random sample of parents being treated in an adult outpatient psychiatric clinic. If the parents of autistic children had severe psychopathology, their MMPI profiles should have been similar to those of psychiatric patients. Instead, MMPI profiles of parents of autistic children were similar to those of a random sample of parents attending a child guidance clinic. Goldfarb, Spitzer, and Endicott (1976) also failed to demonstrate differences in psychopathology and functioning among parent groups.

DeMyer, Barton, and Norton (1972) found through interviews that parents of autistic children and those of extensively matched normal children did not differ in infant acceptance, warmth, nurturing, feeding, and tactile or general stimulation. In contrast, Massie (1978), using home movies taken before age 6 months, judged that mothers of mixed-type child psychotics showed less adequate eye gaze and infant touching than normal controls. Feeding measures for the two infant groups were judged not to differ. On the face of it, Massie's findings offer support for the nurture-causation theory of child psychosis, but low rater correlations (.39 to .54) and important variations in film segments cast doubt on the adequacy of the method (DeMyer, Hingtgen, and Jackson 1981). In addition, Cantwell, Baker, and Rutter (1979) demonstrated that parent–child interactions of families with autistic and dysphasic children were similar in quality and intensity except that the autistic children received more interactions.

After reviewing recent family research, McAdoo and DeMyer (1978b) concluded that, as a group, parents of autistic children display no more signs of mental or emotional illness than parents whose children have organic disorders with or without psychosis. Also, they do not have extreme personality traits, such as coldness, obsessiveness, social anxiety, or rage, nor do they possess specific deficits in infant and child care.

It is of interest to note that, in both England and the United States (Cox et al. 1975; DeMyer 1979), evidence was found that rearing an autistic child commonly produced stressful and depressive symptoms in mothers who had struggled unsuccessfully for months to years to socialize them. DeMyer (1979) found that, before pregnancy with the affected child, mental illness was no more common in parents of autistic children than in a well-matched normal control group. Fathers as a group were less expressive of their emotions, but nevertheless were deeply affected, saying that their wives' emotional pain in turn depressed them and they worried about the ultimate effects of the continuing stress.

Attempts to find familial and social environmental triggering sources for autism continue to be reported in the literature. At the interpersonal levels, stressors can be influential. But the facts suggest that prenatal physiological stressors, which may operate either on their own or in combination with a genetic predisposition, are more decisive.

Autism *has* occurred in children with untreated phenylketonuria, congenital rubella syndrome, celiac disease, and chemical exposure during gestation, but many cases cannot be linked to any of these putative causes. Here, genetic studies may help. Indeed, behind these etiologic factors we could expect to find predisposing or loading factors (Ritvo 1981). For example, a defect in the inborn genetic resistance to infections would be a loading factor if it allowed an infection to reach the brain, which could then cause pathology and lead to autistic behavior. If we use Freedman's (1971a) discussion of genetics and schizophrenia as a conceptual paradigm, it appears that in genotypes with low loading for autism, sustained trauma at some neurophysiological level may lead to phenotypic autism of a milder variety. In another way, individuals with a high genetic loading for autism appear capable of developing more severe degrees of autism in a relatively trauma-free environment.

There is evidence that both biological and environmental factors are simultaneously operating to produce autism (Ritvo 1981). We must ask, then, in what percentage of autistic cases does exogenous congenital central nervous system damage play a role? Presumably brain-damaged autistic children might be considered phenocopies[3] of the remaining nonorganic percentage, who, in this hypothesis, exhibit substantial genetic loading.

In spite of the great advantages afforded humans by genetic variability, many genes maintained in natural populations may be disadvantageous to their carriers, either in certain combination or in homozygous condition. The extent to which a population departs from a perfect genetic constitution is the genetic load. This is the negative side of the theory that regards these genes as mainsprings of evolution. Still, a mutated gene that is harmful in the environment in which the species lives may become useful or even essential if the environment changes.

Perhaps the most intensively studied example of this process is the mutation that gives rise to the sickle-cell trait. In an environment where malaria is prevalent, the genotype with the sickle-cell trait can enjoy essentially normal health with a 1% to 15% chance of surviving invasion by the most dangerous malarial parasites. One genotype with the sickle-cell trait also carries sickle-cell anemia. Thus a gene may be good from an evolutionary standpoint but fatal to the individual.

There is some evidence that autism is an interplay between individuals and populations. Autism is associated with high intelligence (Rimland 1964), perhaps as part of the genetic load or susceptibility to central nervous system damage that the human race accepts in exchange for obtaining some individuals of very high intelligence. Parents of autistic children are frequently of above-average intelligence, and both highly intelligent and autistic children are overrepresented among firstborns, males, and Jews. Should we give serious consideration, then, to the hypothesis that an infant's road to intelligence lies along a knife-edged path, and the higher the potential intelligence the steeper and more precarious the slope (Rimland 1964)? Autism is, so to speak, a price paid by the family and the breeding population for the creative phenotypes associated with it (Freedman 1979).

Unless the biological theories of autism are inaccurate, none of these data militate against a psychotherapeutic approach to symptom alleviation. (See Freedman [1971a] for a case of psychotherapeutic intervention with a schizophrenic child.) Since an illustration of psychotherapy with an autistic child can be of heuristic value, I present in *Case Studies in Autism: A Young Child and Two Adolescents* (Seifert 1990a), the case history of Brian.

Brian was a 7-year-old boy diagnosed with infantile autism at 3 years of age. He exhibited many characteristic symptoms of a biological etiology: mild motor involvement, delays in developmental milestones, and marked discrepancies between abilities. His case, which showed improvement through a psychotherapeutic approach, supports the thesis that presumed organicity does not rule out psychotherapy and that effective psychotherapy does not depend on viewing the environment as the primary source of pathology. Clancy and McBride (1969) state it well (see also Chapter 8):

> In view of these observations, we are forced to conclude that a range of defects is present from the earliest days of life, and that there is a regular progression in the development of the syndrome. . . .
>
> We present a theoretical model of autism as a developmental process operating within a social system, the family. Kanner (1943) originally suggested that the autistic child is born with a congenital inability to form bonds. Our experience shows that these children can form affiliations and we suggest that the initial defect operates to interfere with the process by which bonds form. We see the child and his family, particularly the mother, contributing mutually to this abnormal affiliative process, so that the child is incorporated into the family system in such a way that the autistic process is reinforced and promoted. We suggest that predisposing and initiating factors may be involved in establishing the autistic process which then effectively isolates the child on his own terms. This is seen in the child's active resistance to intrusion by others, the maternal feelings of rejection, the use of "cut-off" behaviours by the child, and the development of a high degree of manipulative skill in ordering his world. We have outlined a régime of treatment based upon this view of autism. The family, rather than the child, is the unit of treatment. Treatment aims at developing a system of family bonds which includes the child and provides the framework for normal socialization. (p. 243)

In the study of Brian, his parents and I acknowledged that they were not to blame for autism. The notion of biological etiology eases the parents' potential guilt and significantly reduces the possibility of a negative feedback circuit (Goldstein 1959) between parents and child.

> All the love the mother can give to the child may not be effective, not only because the infant himself cannot react to it adequately, but also because the mother in turn will not react appropriately if she perceives the child's behavior as inadequate. (p. 555)

Gradually, the physiological deficits that produce such an inadequate infant are being recognized; the treatment recommended varies according to the physiological system in fashion at the time. Ritvo et al. (1986), for example, have examined the possibility of a biochemical basis of autism in which elevated levels of serotonin, a constituent of blood platelets and a neurotransmitter within the central nervous system, is seen as the primary cause. This is not to depreciate the psychological approach, however. What is important is that psychologists and neurophysiologists work cooperatively in careful longitudinal studies of high-risk offspring to bring together coexisting bodies of knowledge.

Sexual Dimorphism

That sex differences exist in the human species is an indisputable biological fact (Hutt 1972).[4] Sexual dimorphism in Homo sapiens is even more pronounced than in many other primates:

> Humans are rather more dimorphic in body-mass than chimpanzees, and much more dimorphic than any other hominoid in the development of epigamic characters, especially on the breast and about the head and neck, which can only be paralleled, in primates, in some baboons. Equally, there seems little to suggest that human males are any less competitive and aggressive among themselves than those of other species; the difference rather lies in the fact that these attributes are expressed in culturally-determined channels . . . rather than by species-specific threat gestures or physical assault, so that expression of rage is postponed and channelled, not abolished at source. (Jolly 1970, p. 7)

The distinctive male or female development in human beings begins at the moment of conception. The 22 pairs of chromosomes that are alike in males and females are called autosomes. The 23rd pair of chromosomes are the sex chromosomes, consisting of XX in the female and XY in the male. The X-chromosome is quite large, about seventh in descending order of size. The Y-chromosome, on the other hand, is very small—often smaller than the smallest autosome. It is the Y-chromosome that organizes sexual differentiation according to a particular pattern. In the absence of a Y-chromosome, feminine development takes place. Apparently the X-chromosome does not play any active role in directing specific sexual development. It seems that nature has provided that, when the equipment necessary for masculine differentiation is lacking, development proceeds according to a female pattern. The Y-chromosome, for instance, not only determines masculinity but confers male traits on human development (Thompson and Thompson 1986).

On average, 120 males are conceived for every 100 females. At term, the ratio is 110 males to 100 females: in live births, the ratio decreases to 106 males to 100 females. This means that the majority of spontaneous abortions or miscarriages, many of which are due to chromosomal abnormalities, are of male fetuses. Male infants are also more susceptible to perinatal complications such as lack of oxygen. Throughout life the human male remains more vulnerable to a variety of disorders, including cerebral palsy, febrile convulsions, viral infections, ulcers, and coronary thrombosis, which curtail longevity to the degree that the sex ratio is reversed by the sixth and seventh decades of life in favor of females (Potts 1970).

Among the consequences of having different sex-chromosomes in males and females is the males' greater susceptibility to recessive disorders. There being only one X-chromosome in the male, all defective genes on the X-chromosome will be manifest, even recessive ones; whereas the female, because one X-chromosome is inactivated in each cell, will be a functional mosaic of X-borne genes. This may explain the greater number of male than female autistic children (4:1) and higher male in utero mortality. That more males than females are conceived in many species is nature's way of ensuring an adequate number of surviving males.

SUMMARY

A theory that attempts to account for individual differences in either biological structure or behavior must recognize the facts of genetic variation. Similarly, a theoretical system that focuses on the individual life span—for example, psychoanalysis—is limited insofar as it precludes the population concepts of modern biology. Evolutionary theory, while it begins with population concepts, in the final analysis can enfold the facts of a typological system such as psychoanalysis (Freedman, Loring, and Martin 1967). The development of parent-child interaction is understood here to involve phylogenetically programmed needs and reactions in both parents and child.

The evolutionary perspective does not deny the environment's importance, "for in phylogeny as well as in ontogeny we must posit an environment of evolutionary adaptedness, that is, an environment to which a species has become phylogenetically adapted" (Freedman 1971a, p. 261). Pathology can involve a lack in either the organism, the environment, or both.

Freedman (1971a) cites evidence from one case that shows pathology in "attachment patterns" resulting from an infant having been raised in an orphanage; in another case he shows mental retardation resulting from the untreated genetic disorder, phenylketonuria. In the first case, pathology stems from an inadequate environment in which the normal actualization[5] of a genetically intact organism is hindered; in the second case pathology results from a genetic defect in which phenylketonuria prevents normal interaction with an adequate environment. In both cases, therapy is possible: through provision of a mother substitute in the first example, and, in the second, by controlling the amount of phenylalanine in the diet.

The discovery that autism is associated with cerebellar vermal hypoplasia (Courchesne et al. 1988) suggests there is no longer any doubt that autism reflects a developmental neurobiological disorder. The results indicate that autism is strongly associated with anatomical abnormalities of the cerebellum. The more promising statement on autism will consider genetics and start with the basic premise presented here, that both genetic defect and environmental triggering mechanisms play important roles. I found in *Case Studies in Autism: A Young Child and Two Adolescents* (Seifert 1990a) that choosing between the two was not necessary. Heredity and environment can be co-appreciated within a biological explanation of autism.

4

Piaget's Analysis of Intelligence

In the search for a theoretical framework for understanding autistic intelligence, developmental approaches help by establishing successive "stages"—defined as the outcome of a process of qualitative differentiation or evolution in form. Piaget ([1936] 1952) theorizes that self-regulation occurs through adaptation, in which selective interactions are incorporated into patterns of behavior and intellectual structures adapted to cope with environmental stress. Piaget's emphasis on internal structure seems almost to deny the weight of external factors such as the social environment. This is evident in his predominantly cognition-bound theories and infrequent reference to unique personalities or emotional involvement, to the point of taking affect out of affect. In spite of his voluminous recorded observations of children, Piaget failed to observe that infants smile almost exclusively at people rather than objects, a response that serves primarily social adaptation.[1]

Nevertheless, Piaget's stage theory of intellectual development is helpful in locating a child's level of growth. The theory states that the development of children's intelligence occurs in stages of invariant sequence, which stem originally from motor action but progress by a complex process of reconstruction to increasingly sophisticated mental functions. Piaget's concern is with the development of intelligence, not with the appearance of an item of behavior nor with the age at which it appears (Piaget [1947] 1950, [1936] 1952, [1937] 1954). His ([1947] 1950) concern is limited to defining the child's three main developmental stages: sensorimotor, lasting from birth to 2 years; concrete operations, from 2 to 12 years; and formal operations, from 12 years through adulthood.

SENSORIMOTOR STAGE

The sensorimotor stage is one in which the infant predominantly relies on sensory and body motor experiences. The main developmental goals for this period are coordinating motor activities and organizing sensory perception into a whole. Piaget ([1936] 1952) subdivides this period into six substages of organization that build upon one another. These substages present a progression from spontaneous movements and reflexes to acquired habits, and ultimately to intelligence. The mechanism of this progression is the process of assimilation—the process whereby the infant organizes substances and energies in his environment so they can be incorporated into the organization of his life and mental activity.

The first substage of the sensorimotor stage is the *use of reflexes*. At this stage, the infant assimilates his environment according to his organic needs. Two phases can be seen: generalized assimilation, in which the infant indiscriminately incorporates more objects from within his immediate environment, and recognition assimilation, in which he begins to differentiate objects in an environment previously undifferentiated.

The second substage, in which voluntary movement slowly replaces reflexive behavior, is referred to as *primary circular reactions*. These occur around the second month; the infant voluntarily repeats behavior that was previously automatic. Here the infant incorporates and adapts his responses to his environment. This deliberate response to a recognized stimulus signals the emergence of an accommodation process whereby the infant begins adapting to the requirements of his environment.

During this substage the infant develops sensorimotor schemata. A schema, in Piaget's system, is a sensorimotor concept referring to a group of similar action sequences in an organized totality. Schemata and concepts are similar but not synonymous. Schema is a motor equivalent to a system of relations and classes that is basic to further development of preconcepts and, ultimately, concepts. When vision becomes a continuous experience, eye–hand coordination emerges. Two new areas of organization appear at this substage: a notion of causality and a notion of temporal space. The infant's first understanding of causality is his recognition of the connection between an action and a result, for example, obtaining food as an extension of sucking or grasping. The notion of temporal space develops through awareness of a sequence of experienced events.

The third substage of the sensorimotor stage is called *secondary circular reactions*. Circular reaction patterns (such as reproducing interesting events that were initially discovered by chance in the external environment) are continued in this stage but combined with a secondary function that gives them a purpose beyond basic organic activity. The goal at this substage is retention, not repetition. Primary circular reactions are prolonged by the new secondary reactions. For example, the grasping reflex, a primary circular reaction, now moves from grasping and holding to a shaking, pulling, or tugging activity. The child uses similar means to achieve different ends. The presence of a new toy on top of the cradle will stimulate the same behavior that was exhibited when the old toy was there. This use of the same behavior for different purposes is the beginning of intelligence.

The fourth substage appears near the child's first birthday and is the period of development in which secondary circular reactions are applied to new situations. Using previous behavioral achievements to develop new ones, the child experiments with different ways of dealing with the objects he encounters. Unlike previous stages, the coordination of means and ends is new in each situation, but the means used are based on previous schemata. This can be seen in hide-and-seek situations when an object has been hidden behind a pillow and is then found by the infant. The combination is new, but the act of grasping and moving the pillow relates to a habitual schema.

In the first half of the second year, the fifth substage, referred to as *tertiary circular reactions,* occurs. Experimentation at this stage entails a search for new approaches by differentiating these from schemata already known. For example, an infant trying in vain to grasp an object on a rug may hold the corner of the rug and pull it toward him to gain the object.

Finally, the sixth substage indicates the end of the sensorimotor period and a transition to what Piaget ([1936] 1952) refers to as the stage of invention of new means through *mental combinations*. In this stage, the child develops new means of achieving a goal by synthesizing external and internal combinations to form a sudden comprehension or insight. In one of Piaget's favorite examples of behavior at this stage, he describes a child confronted by a slightly open matchbox containing a thimble. The child first tries to open the box by physical groping (similar to the fifth substage), but upon failing, he presents an altogether new reaction: he stops the action and attentively examines the situation (in the course of this he slowly opens and closes his mouth), after which he suddenly slips his finger into the crack and thus succeeds in opening the box. The appearance of insight or comprehension at this stage results from development in previous stages. This substage is therefore not separate from the others but signals their completion.

Development during the sensorimotor stage lays the foundation for further cognition. The importance of the sensorimotor schemata that develop during this stage is emphasized in a study reported by Piaget and Inhelder ([1966] 1969). They compare the emergence of logic in deaf-mute children (Borelli 1951; Oléron 1961; Vincent 1956) who were in possession of complete sensorimotor schemata but did not have the benefit of articulate language, with that of blind children (Hatwell's study, cited in Piaget and Inhelder ([1966] 1969) who had the benefit of articulate language but not the complete sensorimotor schemata, and with normal children who had both skills. The results indicate that, compared with normal children, blind children are delayed up to four years in understanding relationships of order (succession, position, "between," etc.) and other concepts reflecting the emergence of logic. Deaf children, compared with normal children, also showed a delay. The delay was not considered significant, however, because deaf children enact the same developmental stages as normal children, but one or two years later. It appears, then, that the verbal skills of the blind children were not sufficient to compensate for the sensory handicap that interfered with their developing sensorimotor schemata and general coordination. Apparently, action learning is necessary for these children to master higher operation functions similar to those of normal children.

CONCRETE OPERATIONAL STAGE

The mechanisms in use during the sensorimotor phase are prerepresentational, which means that the ability to represent an absent object is not present until the second year, when the child enters the second stage of Piaget's ([1947] 1950) hierarchy, the *concrete operational stage*. During this stage semiotic or symbolic functions appear that are basic to all further cognitive development. Piaget and Inhelder ([1966]

1969) define the semiotic function as "the ability to represent something by means of a signifier which is differentiated and which serves only a representative purpose: language, mental image, symbolic gesture" (p. 51). During the concrete operations stage, symbols are constructed, concepts of space, causality, and time are acquired, and thought becomes decentered from perception and action, permitting such activities as classifying, ordering, and numbering. The final period of formal operations envelopes the systematization and recombination of the concrete operations in which the logical structures of abstract thought and reasoning are mastered. Thus, development moves from perception of the concrete to abstract thinking.

The presence of Piaget and Inhelder's ([1966] 1969) semiotic function, which constitutes the representational process, has implications for the study of autism where speech fails to develop. Could this be the stage in which the autistic child's learning breaks down? The autistic child's mental development is arrested at the sensorimotor stage of infancy and does not progress to the concrete operational stage.

The Semiotic Function

Piaget and Inhelder ([1966] 1969) identify five simultaneously developing behavioral patterns that suggest the presence of the semiotic function and are necessary for its development. These are (1) deferred imitation, (2) symbolic play, (3) drawing a graphic image, (4) the mental image, and (5) the verbal evocation of events. Piaget and Inhelder's ([1966] 1969) identification of drawing as contributing to the development of the representation process has especial value in explicating human-figure drawings. Drawing, which serves the nonverbal child as a readily accessible means of communication, can be used for psychodiagnosis as well. For this reason, drawings seem to be a useful, objective means for studying autism (Seifert 1990b) and an obvious vehicle for presenting a case history (Seifert 1990a).

Piaget and Inhelder ([1966] 1969) state that a relationship exists between the graphic image made by the child and his internal image. Reporting on research by Luquet (1927), who studied children's drawings, they conclude that although the child's early drawings are intended to be realistic, the child draws what he knows about the stimulus rather than what he actually sees. If drawings are more a reflection of what a child knows or conceptualizes than of what he perceives, one can see why tests evaluating a child's drawings are helpful in determining his cognitive development in the area of representation. Often the autistic child has difficulty initially performing the human-figure drawing tests, possibly due to his poor internal imaging. Because the internal images are not clear, he is unable to make a graphic representation, even though he perceives the model he attempts to copy.

The consequences, then, of immature or faulty semiotic functions would be critical to a child's ability to develop subsequent language. He would have grave problems establishing representations by symbols and even more difficulty establishing representations by arbitrary signs. The symptoms of this deficit would be evident in problems of receptive and expressive language.

Let us consider the consequences of a deficit in the semiotic function and see if this represents the syndrome of the autistic child. The process of representation must involve the process of abstraction, as it is impossible to represent something in its entirety. In other words, the child must be able first to internalize his abstracted detail, if he is to represent it as a mental image. Let us assume the autistic child cannot do this. It follows that his entire world will then be unstructured. Since he will not be able to abstract important details, he will find his environment confusing. His inability to abstract will prevent him from representing his experiences and thus making them meaningful. Having no representation of reality, he will not be able to distinguish between what is real and what is unreal. His inability to function at the beginning levels of representation will interfere with his ability to use the arbitrary signs of language. His ability to understand language will be distorted, and this in turn will interfere with his expressive language skills at all levels. The above is typical of many children diagnosed as having infantile autism.

Although Piaget and Inhelder ([1966] 1969) believe that language is not necessary for the initial development of thought, they stress its role in conceptual thinking. They state that language is the vehicle par excellence of symbolization; without language thought could never become socialized and, thereby, logical. Without a doubt, Piaget and Inhelder consider language necessary for the development of higher levels of thinking. A child's inability to express the experiences he has internalized would be analogous to his having boxes of stored food and no way of getting into them. (See Chapter 5 for further discussion of language and thought.)

Since language is also essential to social development, the autistic child's social skills are, understandably, severely limited. Luria (1961) theorizes that speech performs a central role in organizing human behavior and, specifically, in regulating higher forms of behavior. One only has to bring to mind the problem-solving ability and conceptualization present in the cases of Helen Keller,[2] the deaf, mute, and blind child who suddenly discovered meaning in the word, and Viktor, Itard's ([1801, 07] 1932, 62) 19th-century *Wild Boy of Aveyron,* who lived with animals in the woods until he became civilized, to be impressed with Luria's conclusions concerning the regulative, stabilizing, and mediating functions speech plays in intelligent human behavior.

Piaget and Inhelder ([1966] 1969) discuss two differences between verbal and sensorimotor behavior that have implications for the autistic child. One is that sensorimotor patterns are bound to experience because such reactions cannot exceed the speed of action. Verbal patterns, however, can very rapidly represent a long chain of actions. If the cognitive development of the autistic child is arrested at the sensorimotor stage, it would be understandable that he is unable to relate experiences. Case histories of these autistic children often reflect parental complaints that the children do not tell of their experiences at school or at play. Because they can express only a single need pertaining to immediate experience, these children seem limited to the event they are involved in.

Second, Piaget and Inhelder ([1966] 1969) state that sensorimotor behavior is bound to the immediate space and time, whereas verbal behavior allows thought to be liberated from the present. Could it be that the autistic child's inability to comprehend past, present, and future in relation to each other results from poor verbal skills? Autistic children are bound to the present and confused by concepts of before and after. Generally, Piaget and Inhelder state that sensorimotor intelligence proceeds step by step, whereas verbal intelligence can simultaneously present all the steps involved.

The advantages of representational thought are the result of the semiotic function. This function is the source of representation and liberates thought from action. If the absence of the semiotic function creates the language problems of the autistic child, then it is understandable why he is so bound to the concrete, to the immediate, to only that which is displayed in front of him. The autistic child has great difficulty reaching the concrete operational stage of development. In fact, at each level he has such difficulties to overcome it is very unlikely he will reach the last stage of cognitive development.

The Representational Deficit

Piaget's ([1947] 1950, [1936] 1952, [1937] 1954) and Piaget and Inhelder's ([1966] 1969) hierarchy of cognitive development has significant implications for infantile autism. Their identification of the semiotic function as a system for representation suggests that a child's ability and capacity to represent is not based on language, but the reverse, the child's language is based on the capacity of the representational system. It seems, then, that looking at the autistic child through his language abilities would not be as beneficial as studying his total process of cognitive development. According to Piaget and Inhelder ([1966] 1969), verbal capacity is the final acquisition of the semiotic function. If so, then examining the autistic child's language first would lead only to a surface understanding of his problems; whereas a total evaluation of cognitive development, emphasizing semiotic and representation processes would serve as a better basis for diagnostic conclusions.

Again, according to Piaget and Inhelder ([1966] 1969), such an evaluation of the representational process should include a study of the child's imitation and deferred imitation abilities, his ability to partake in symbolic play, and his ability to make graphic images, as well as an evaluation of his ability to use verbal signs. An evaluation of all these areas—prerequisites to good verbal language skills—should indicate at what level the child is breaking down. The autistic child often has problems in all of these areas. We might therefore begin examining such children's imitation abilities, symbolic play, ability to make graphic images, and ability to use verbal signs that build a foundation for representation, rather than beginning with diagnostic and therapeutic techniques directed toward language.

5

Language and Thought in Autism

This chapter attempts to derive implications about autism from the relationship between language and thought. Piaget's position is that the child's language reflects his logic and that the mere acquisition of vocabulary will have little effect on thought processes. His theory holds that cognitive structures are consistently reinforced by the syntactic structure of language but not determined by it.

Furth (1961, 1964) takes Piaget's view when he proposes that the difficulty of appraising the contribution of language to the development of thinking results from their appearing to develop simultaneously. Like Piaget, he contends that cognitive capacity involves more than language. Language is the vehicle by which thought is socialized and thus made logical, but is not the original basis of, nor does it ever become, the whole of human thinking. The process of conceptualization is dependent, rather, on experiences obtained directly through interaction with the environment.

CONCEPTUALIZATION IN THE DEAF

To demonstrate the relatively independent processes of language and thinking, Furth studied conceptualization in the deaf; their language deficiency makes them uniquely suited for examining the influence of language on thought.

Furth (1961) conducted three experiments with 180 deaf and hearing children, ages 7 to 12, to demonstrate that the deaf person's capacity to deal with conceptual tasks is not generally retarded or impaired.

Task 1, *sameness,* required the subjects to determine whether two figures were the same.

43

Task 2, *symmetry,* involved recognizing symmetrical and asym-
metrical figures.
Task 3, *opposition,* consisted of acquiring concepts of extremes,
e.g., largest, smallest.

Furth hypothesized that the hearing subjects would exhibit more
successful performance only on the third task, in which access to a
particular word would increase the efficiency of problem solving. As
expected, little difference was noted between the performances of deaf
and hearing subjects on the sameness and symmetry tasks, but hearing
subjects were superior on the opposition experiment, leading Furth to
conclude that the influence of language on concept formation is ex-
trinsic and specific. Language, he believes, cannot be assumed to be a
prerequisite for the development of a capacity to abstract and generalize.

It is important to understand that the term *language* here refers to
"the living language as heard and spoken in our society. Knowing a
language means mastery of a particular language so that its structure
and vocabulary are implicitly understood and employed by a person"
(Furth 1961, p. 386). The deaf, then, are considered deficient in language only to the extent that they lack a readily available verbal me-
dium with which to communicate. Designating the deaf as having a
language deficit is not to say they lack capacity for conceptual and
symbolic behavior. Language, in this instance spoken, refers to the
vehicle for transmitting or communicating symbols representing concepts. Furth's conclusion, drawn from the above experiments, indicates that linguistic habits facilitate but are not a prerequisite for conceptual thinking.

Oléron (1953) reported on three experiments conducted with deaf
children, observing that the deaf experienced difficulty in conceptual
thinking, as demonstrated by their performance on classification tasks.
The three experiments required the subjects to abstract a principle of
classification, i.e., to form a concept.

The first experiment, conducted by Höfler (1927), used the Weigl
Sorting Test in which classification was possible by attributes of color
or function. The Weigl Color-Form Sorting Test (Weigl 1941) consists
of four small plastic squares, four triangles, and four circles, each
reproduced in one of four colors. The subject is asked to sort them into
groups (form a concept, e.g., color) and then resort them in a different
way (form a second concept, e.g., form). It was observed that at all

age levels, the deaf subjects demonstrated behavior characteristics of attachment to a single aspect and an inability to achieve an alternative grouping.

A second experiment by MacAndrew (1948), requiring the subjects to execute two possible categories (form and substance), obtained results similar to those observed by Höfler: sorting was based on one attribute only, despite preliminary training exercises intended to facilitate alternative classifications.

Oléron similarly noted in a third experiment that the subjects were unable to execute sorting by alternatives of object representation, color, or number, although the examiner initiated new categories following the subjects' spontaneous grouping.

These experiments demonstrate that the deaf have difficulty shifting classification, leading some to theorize that Goldstein and Scheerer's (1941) "concrete attitude" may accurately describe the deaf's conceptual abilities: objects are perceived as things having individual differences, not as representative of a category or class. Oléron, however, rejected implications of rigidity in the mental structure of the deaf. Instead, he suggests a theory invoking two prerequisites for conceptual ability. The first, a perceptive condition, requires that the perceptible qualities of objects be recognized; the second, a conceptual condition, allows grouping to be achieved by common classification. For sorting activities to take place at a conceptual level, the perceptive conditions must be subordinated to conceptual conditions. Although the perceived characteristics—for example, red, blue—function as an index to grouping, actual grouping depends on grasping the concept of color.

Failure of deaf subjects to perform successive groupings is believed to result from an inability to subordinate the observed elements to the concept; instead, the elements are abstracted as independent entities. On this basis, Oléron regards the cognitive capacity of the deaf as being at an infraconceptual level where the perceptive condition predominates.

Oléron substantiated this interpretation through an examination of verbal behavior following spontaneous sorting tasks by the deaf, noting that a descriptive attitude predominated in subjects' verbally stated reasons for grouping, and the idea of a common class was rarely expressed. Referring to the work of Höfler (1927), which demonstrated that the Weigl Sorting Test was executed better by those subjects with language, Oléron proposed that the attainment of conceptualization depends on a knowledge of and ability to use abstract terms. Language would therefore be significant and fundamental in its contribution to conceptual thinking.

At this point, application of Oléron's theory may clarify the results of Furth's (1961) study on the conceptual ability of the deaf. In light of Oléron's identification of a perceptive and conceptual condition, the tasks of sameness and symmetry in Furth's study may evaluate perceptual (discrimination) rather than conceptual ability. Furth's study did not involve sorting activities according to sameness, or grouping on the basis of symmetry, but utilized cards presenting two figures to be differentiated as same or different. Hence, both tasks, following Oléron's definition for a perceptive condition, may be categorized as perceptual. Furth's third task, opposition, more clearly represents a conceptual task, and language-experience was designated as a necessary condition for adequate performance.

Another investigation of the conceptual abilities of the deaf obtained results indicating support for a language-oriented theory. Blank and Bridger (1966) compared the performance of hearing and deaf children in cross-modal transfer of (1) the concept *something* versus *nothing* using 3- to 5-year-olds and (2) number concepts using 5- and 6-year-olds. The younger deaf and hearing subjects exhibited equally poor performances, which the authors interpreted as failure of the hearing subjects to use available language in directing their problem solving, resulting in stimulus-bound responses. The authors related the results to language ability, noting that the successful performances demonstrated by both deaf and hearing subjects were, in the older group, facilitated by language.

The statements offered by Blank and Bridger for demonstrating conceptualization correspond to Oléron's perceptive and conceptual conditions. The perceptual performance of younger deaf and hearing subjects in adopting fixed or stimulus-bound patterns of response may be interpreted as their functioning at a perceptual level, while older deaf and hearing subjects operate at a conceptual level. The authors further clarify the issue of language versus nonlanguage in conceptual ability by identifying the role of language as one of generating symbols that permit the individual to manipulate concepts and operate within the context of a nonpresent reality.

The extent, then, to which an individual can symbolize an object, an event, or experience determines his ability to deal conceptually with the materials presented him. It would appear that the ability of the deaf to demonstrate conceptual capacity depends on a representational process, and it is this ability that identifies success in classification tasks. Ability to symbolize or to represent is not synonymous with language but may be fundamental to its acquisition. Symbolization operates at Oléron's conceptual level and signifies in deaf children evidence of concept attainment. Conceptual thought will be adversely affected to the degree that a representational process depends on overt language for higher levels of abstraction. Abstract levels of classification, e.g., furniture, animals, are seldom attained by the deaf because they lack the word. The deaf, then, are to be considered not only less efficient, but also deficient, in concept formation.

NORMAL CONCEPTUAL DEVELOPMENT

Discussion of conceptual development is offered by Siegel (1953), based on a study with 60 children, ages 7, 9, and 11. The experiment was designed to determine classifying behavior with increasing age, using five variants of the test situation:

1. tactual-motor, in which the subjects were allowed to handle the objects while establishing groups;
2. visual nonmotor, using the same objects but with the subjects indicating groupings to be made by the examiner;
3. pictures of the objects to be grouped;
4. names of each object printed on cards for the subjects to group manually; and
5. names of objects listed on a sheet of paper and the subjects required to write the group.

Spontaneous groupings were followed with a request that the subjects explain the basis for establishing each group. The subjects were then encouraged to group "the things that are alike or belong together into fewer groupings than you made the first time," until the number of groups could not be reduced further. Reasons for groupings followed each trial.

Groups were classified as perceptual, conceptual, or miscellaneous. Groups considered and scored conceptual had to be treated as members of a class and a class name supplied, even though gross structural differences were apparent. Results indicate that regardless of the nature of the material, classification on a perceptual basis decreased, and conceptual classification increased, with age. Siegel noted that the younger subjects appeared to perceive the materials in terms of specific elements and, once having established a classification, were unable to employ higher levels of abstraction or offer alternatives.

Changes in ability to deal conceptually with material at different age levels may relate to a developing symbol system that allows flexibility in thinking. Devising groups dependent on more abstract categories requires that the individual impose organization on the material in deliberately conceived categories, and for this a symbol is necessary.

O'Connor and Hermelin (1959) studied symbols as a stabilizer for concepts and a means by which experience is systematized. The study, conducted on severely subnormal children, later supported Luria's (1961) theory that language assumes a directive function over behavior. Response patterns that develop without verbal association are believed to be extremely unstable and disintegrate whenever a slight change occurs in the manner of presenting the signals.

The initial phase of their study required that the subjects shift to learning a previously negative stimulus (reversal learning), e.g., *smaller, larger*. Of the ten institutionalized and ten normal subjects, eight of the normal subjects but none of the subnormal subjects verbalized size as the basis of selection, indicating their incapacity to use size as a basis for problem solving. The authors theorize that normal subjects tend to formulate a solution through verbal self-instructions: words guide their hypothesis regarding the correct response, which stabilizes the concept of larger or smaller size. Invoking verbal mediation creates a conflict when the alternative to the original response is reinforced, indicating that a concept has been stabilized. The subnormal subjects' responses indicate reinforcement from the immediate stimulus.

The second phase of their study repeated the reversal learning task with another group of ten subjects identified as imbeciles. This group received verbal input to stabilize their response pattern. The results tend to support the theory that lack of verbal regulation results in unstable responses that could be rapidly reversed.

Other investigations into the role of verbal mediation in conceptual learning support the theory that familiarity with a symbol facilitates learning (Cantor 1955; Phyles 1932; Thompson 1941). Results of different studies indicate that, with age, children's conceptual capacity is increasingly characterized by verbal mediation skills dependent on the ability to represent material symbolically.

REPRESENTATIONAL DEFICITS LIMIT CONCEPTUALIZATION

The above studies show a correlation between language development and conceptual ability. In relating these findings to autism, we can postulate that the breakdown of language development lies in the child's inability to represent and integrate experiences in a conceptual process by means of symbols. Symbols organize, stabilize, and allow for transmission of thought; lack of ability to symbolize is a central processing disorder that prevents organized thought. The thinking disorder in turn results from an incapacity to denote and categorize experiences so they can be stored, associated, and applied.

> Symbolism is the study of the part played in human affairs by language and symbols of all kinds, and especially of their influence on thought. It singles out for special inquiry the ways in which symbols help us and hinder us in reflecting on things. . . . Symbols direct and organize, record and communicate. . . . It is *thought* . . . which is directed and organized, and it is also thought which is recorded and communicated. (Ogden and Richards 1967, p. 41)

The word, then, is functional only to the degree that it represents material and, through representation, allows knowledge to be apprehended, organized, and transformed.

The conceptual ability of the autistic child may be characterized as lacking in representation. An inability to represent results in a media-

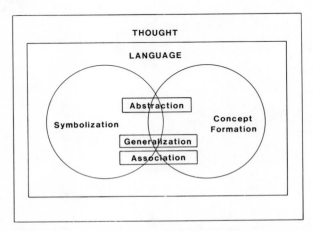

Figure 5-1. Interrelationship of concept formation.

tional deficiency reciprocally affecting the attainment of concepts, a prerequisite for the development of thought. The autistic child, because of his inability to symbolize, is impaired in his conceptual capacity, except perhaps when new concepts are generated at a very low level of abstraction. Investigating the autistic child's conceptual abilities could determine the degree to which he is able to engage in conceptual activity. It may be that in the autistic child concepts can develop only at a perceptual level.

Figure 5-1 represents the interrelationship of concept formation, symbolization, language, and thought. The processes of abstraction, generalization, and association are operative in both concept formation and symbolization. The overlap of concept formation and symbolization designates the integration of the two conceptual processes necessary for developing language and thought. Unjoining these two processes results in a condition in which representation is supplanted by signifiers, here defined as words independent of meaning. A lack of integration in the presence of words or word patterns describes echolalic speech, nearly a specific for a diagnosis of organic brain dysfunction and typical of many autistic children's speech.

6

Aphasias and Autism

Goldstein (1948) described central aphasia in detail, especially as it pertains to adults. But his discussion also has provocative implications for central aphasia in children. Central aphasia is a severe language disorder, characterized by marked deficiencies in receptive and expressive capacities; clinically the child and adult seem devoid of any capacity for symbolic behavior. As Goldstein suggests, this severe disorder seems to derive not only from the combined receptive and expressive incapacities, but also from an additional involvement: a disturbance in inner language function.

To differentiate, expressive aphasia is an impaired capacity to speak to others; receptive aphasia is an impaired capacity to understand what others say; and central aphasia is an impaired capacity to use language for thinking, for "talking to oneself." Goldstein (1948) states that central aphasia involves a brain lesion that is different from, but usually simultaneous with, lesions that cause receptive and expressive aphasias. From this view of differential diagnosis, central aphasia (the most pervasive and handicapping of the three aphasias) presents marked disturbances in all language functions and in general behavior, with extreme deviations of behavioral symptomatology.

MIXED TRANSCORTICAL APHASIA SYNDROME

My review of neurological literature indicates that the clinical picture of mixed transcortical aphasia resembles the language function profile of the autistic syndrome. Both show preserved production of meaningless speech and memorization capability. The neurological syndrome mixed transcortical aphasia (MTA) is described as a rare, fascinating variety of aphasia that has been thoroughly discussed 'by Geschwind, Quadfasel, and Segarra (1968). Two names have been suggested for the syndrome: "isolation of the speech area," emphasizing the clinical picture, and "mixed transcortical aphasia," which recognizes a combination of features of the transcortical motor and transcortical sensory syndromes.

The clinical characteristics are striking: of all language functions, only repetition is preserved. (See Benson's [1979] description of the borderzone aphasic syndromes.) A patient with MTA does not speak unless spoken to, and then his verbal output is almost entirely limited to what has been offered to him—a true echolalia. The patient with MTA may embellish the output somewhat, in the form of the "completion phenomenon." Thus, given the beginning of a common phrase, the patient may repeat what has been said but also continue the phrase to completion. Articulation is clear. Series speech is comparatively good once the patient is prompted in the task. If the patient is started counting, naming the months, or reciting a story, he can continue the activity with ease. If interrupted, he cannot continue, giving one a feeling that the response is automatic, similar to the reading of a passage from an uncomprehended language.

Comprehension of spoken language is severely disturbed in those with MTA. Some patients have, on occasion, demonstrated a degree of comprehension, but comprehension has always been strictly limited. The ability to repeat, while effectively preserved compared to all other language features, remains well below normal. The number of words in a phrase that can be repeated is often limited to three or four. MTA patients repeat common sentences or phrases and may or may not correct grammatically incorrect phrases. They repeat nonsense syllables and foreign words surprisingly accurately. All of these tasks are limited, however, by a short attention span.

MTA patients show severe difficulty in naming, sometimes producing neologisms or semantic paraphasias. Similarly, the ability to read and comprehend what is read and the ability to write are severely disturbed. In an elementary sense, the patient with MTA has a central aphasia, except for the preservation of an ability to repeat what has been said.

The mixed transcortical syndrome appears to occur only in individuals with severe brain damage. The course of the syndrome appears to be stable but without improvement. The total number of cases reported is extremely small.

Despite the limited number of acquired MTA cases recorded in the literature, a variety of pathologies have been reported. Goldstein (1948) postulated that different problems could produce this syndrome. He recorded five cases, two resulting from major cerebral vascular insults and three from diffuse encephalopathy. The case of Geschwind, Quadfasel, and Segarra (1968) was secondary to self-inflicted anoxia. One patient's syndrome observed by Benson (1979) resulted from cerebral edema following trauma to the brain. Two others had suffered acute carotid occlusion. Each variety of pathology described has produced a fairly wide field of pathology. The most intense pathological involvement has been in the vascular border zone of the dominant hemisphere. The case of hypoxia studied at postmortem (Geschwind, Quadfasel, and Segarra 1968) showed rather exact pathology localization in the borderline areas. Similarly, it is conjectured that the etiologies of both carotid occlusion and cerebral edema decrease cerebral oxygen supply, which has a maximal impact on the border-zone area. Thus, the MTA syndrome strongly suggests a locus of pathology involving the cerebral vascular border zone (between the territory of the middle cerebral artery and that of the anterior or posterior cerebral arteries). Life expectancy is not necessarily affected by the disorder.

HYPERLEXIC SYNDROME

Of related interest are cases of the neurological syndrome hyperlexia, evidenced by precocious and compulsive reading against a background of intellectual slowness and autistic behavior. The children call out words on printed material, read aloud, and spell to dictation but cannot understand what they read any better than they understand what is said to them (Elliott and Needleman 1976; Huttenlocher and Huttenlocher 1973). The hyperlexic can name, repeat, and memorize speech sounds but not connect speech sounds with meaning. They can connect visual configurations with speech sounds (name and read aloud) but do not comprehend intralinguistic speech-sound relationships. The clinical picture of the hyperlexic is similar to that described by Heilman, Tucker, and Valenstein in a 1976 adult case of MTA. (See Myklebust's [1978] discussion and definition of dyslexia in which a diagnosis of central aphasia for reading as well as for spoken language is suggested.) The basic language defect seems to be in the association between speech symbols and meaning. In children, the hyperlexic syndrome (Huttenlocher and Huttenlocher 1973) occurs almost exclusively in boys (14 of 15 cases reported) and most likely is caused by a congenital developmental defect.

COMMENT

Drawing upon this research and my clinical experience, I believe there may be a sizable overlap between infantile autism and the brain-based developmental disorder, central aphasia. Moreover, it is quite likely that no single factor underlies all cases; rather, a variety of developmental brain abnormalities and brain injury can lead to the same clinical syndrome. Hauser, DeLong, and Rosman (1975) have made a significant contribution in their report of pathological pneumo-encephalographic findings in the autistic child, in which there was prominent, but not exclusive, enlargement of the left-temporal horn (15 of 18 cases). They state that they were unable to correlate the degree of left-temporal enlargement with clinical severity, but they suspect bilateral lesions, possibly with a left brain preponderance.

It is possible, then, that disconnection, which is not readily visualized anatomically, underlies the isolation characteristic of the infantile autism syndrome with its lack of language comprehension. Instead, there is echolalic repetition and excellent articulation. The report of Hauser, DeLong, and Rosman (1975) discusses this issue. Whether the autistic child's language and social-affective status is best viewed as causally linked (Prior and Bradshaw 1979; Rutter 1974) or as coexisting remains debatable.

7

Human-Figure Drawing as a Projection of Autistic Experience

The psychodiagnostic significance of human-figure drawing in personality projection was established and articulated by Machover (1949). Using psychoanalytic theory and the concept of human-figure drawing as a projection of the internalized body image, she developed a systematic analysis of the child's graphic product. Machover's approach, and a closely related form described by Buck (1948) who asked children to draw a house, a tree, and a person, translated the drawn images into the drawer's postural and psychic tensions. Crucial elements of the drawing—its size, symmetry, and content—and features of the figure were accorded certain symbolic values. Machover's systematic study of the human figure produced a personality portrait of the drawer, stressing interrelated patterns of drawing traits as they might reflect the dynamics of symptom organization in a particular diagnostic category.

Out of combined beginnings, including the use of drawing in the clinical setting, the study of expressive movement in drawing, and the use of drawing as a measure of intelligence, came Machover's (1949) contemporary use of human-figure drawing as a projective device. Goodenough (1926), succeeded by Koppitz (1968), studied large groups of children at different ages and first drew attention to drawings as an indicator of cognitive development and certain pictorial features that appeared related to personality.

The reports of Bender (1937), Bender and Woltmann (1937), Despert (1938), and Bender and Rapaport (1944) broadened our understanding of the significance of drawing and illustrated its use in the clinical setting. Bender's material had the special value of including both normal and pathological states (organically as well as functionally determined). Bender (1937) observed the diagnostic and therapeutic significance of the expressive process during her extensive study of mental disturbances in the children's ward of the Psychiatric Division of Bellevue Hospital, New York. She valued every creation of art without attempting to standardize the conditions of its product and demonstrated the use of children's art as an adjunct to psychotherapy. Bender suggested that drawing was a means of establishing rapport with children and obtaining insight into their unconscious life. She further demonstrated its psychotherapeutic value to the child, claiming cathartic value in the mere opportunity to express unconscious fantasy. She maintained that for the maturing child the expression of motor activity impulses and experimentation with forms, regardless of their ideational content, has therapeutic value as an actualization of a genetically derived capacity in the field of visual motor gestalt function.

Despert (1937a, 1937b) paralleled Bender's work in clinical illustrations and lent support for the use of drawing in the study and treatment of children with emotional problems. In drawings by psychotic children, Despert discovered the concept of regression, as seen in the predominance of characteristics belonging to earlier developmental levels. She described drawing forms of the infantile type, clearly what Krautter (1930) calls the *Kopffüsser,*[1] as well as perseveration and automatism in drawings by psychotic children. She compared the regressions present in those drawings with drawings of neurotic behavior-disordered children and found no evidence of regression in the neurotic children's drawings. Despert concluded that the essential difference between the drawings of psychotic and neurotic children was evidence of regression among those who were psychotic.

Bender (1938, 1949), in a survey of personality projection evaluated in terms of form principles, introduced the importance of understanding normal gestalt functions of the human organism. Recognizing the genetic and temporal factors in perceiving visual form (interacting fields of visual perception and motility), she defined a gestalt function as

> that function of the integrative organism whereby it responds to a given constellation of stimuli as a whole; the response itself being a constellation, or pattern, or gestalt. (1938, p. 3)

Montague (1951) applied Bender's (1938, 1949) theory of gestalt function and Gesell and Amatruda's (1948) developmental stages of sensorimotor action patterns to a study of child schizophrenics' human-figure drawings. She recognized the biophysical origin of the schizophrenic process and demonstrated specific motility and perceptual disturbance in the expressive projection of schizophrenics' drawings. She affirmed that circular loops, the most primitive unit of the visual motor Gestalten, were found in normal children up to the age of 4, whereas in schizophrenic children, some representation of a fluid whirling around a longitudinal axis is common. She substantiated Bender's (1947) original hypothesis that the presence of whirling in children's drawing is nearly a specific for schizophrenic illness, reflecting the unending struggle of the schizophrenic with the inner impulse to whirl.

Rorschach ([1921] 1969) believed that affective experience serves a necessary and independent function for the individual; it gives meaning to life; it colors and moves the form of experience. In a single, rather controversial study in the field of art education (Alschuler and Hattwick 1947), emotionality in children's drawings was directly, though cursorily, discussed. Correlations were drawn between a child's painting and dynamics of personality through an analysis of the use of colors (such as differences in the use of warm and cool colors), line and form, use of space, and spatial patterns. Other art educators, such as Kellogg and O'Dell (1967) and Kellogg (1970), were very receptive to nuances in children's drawings and the growth of their creative spirit.

In summary, the clinical relevance of children's human-figure drawings has been demonstrated as a projective technique for personality study. As such, it is adaptable to a particular theoretical framework— one that encompasses psychodynamic concepts conducive to holism, the study of the full context of behavior.

INTERPRETING CHILDREN'S DRAWINGS

How are children's drawings interpreted? Prinzhorn (1923), referring to Klages (1923), called attention to the concepts of *rhythm* and *rule*, with reference to graphic expressions. When I applied these criteria to discern children's psychodynamic status from their graphic expressions, I found they had a high discriminative power. These simple concepts transcend other attempts at interpretation because they appreciate, in addition to content, the formal elements in children's art productions.

A study of form involves the fundamental elements of human expression that are inherent in expressive movements. In the beginning, there is the pure joy of motion; later, the joy of accomplishment is added. Rhythm, at first a slow and broad sweep, evolves to a finer sense of physical movement. Children have no reason to achieve a definite form when they draw, nor do they interpret the forms they produce. Children who use paper and pencil or paint freely also reveal themselves freely in their expressive movements, particularly in their style of motion. Therefore, children's free artwork provides an opportunity to study their spontaneous expressions, their dynamics. The word *dynamic* pertains to force in motion. Children's expressive movements, standing still in their drawings and paintings, can be determined and measured. At the same time, static graphic elements have the possibility of becoming dissolved again and of being treated as fluid motion (Elkisch 1945).

I studied a sample of drawings and paintings from 1,694 school-age children to gain insight into the individual child's typical way of expressing himself in free artwork. The children's chronological ages were between 3 and 18 years. To study more closely a child's characteristic expression, 12 pictures from nine boys and three girls in the group were selected and photographed (Figs. 7-1 through 7-12). Definitions of rhythm and rule, concepts reflected in these drawings, will be helpful as a general guide for interpreting other drawings. They aim at revealing the psychological and intellectual attitudes inherent in the child's expressive movements, relationship to space, and experience of an outer and inner world. The 12 pictures are by children between ages 6 and 12.

Children's drawings have changed in interesting ways over the past 40 years. When we compare the contemporary drawings presented here to older samples of children's art (Lowenfeld 1954), we readily detect an evolution of subjective emotional states. The contemporary drawings are more sophisticated with respect to complex motor activity, graphic expression, and cognition—expressions that are largely dependent on the child's ability to imitate at a given stage of development. The following samples also suggest implications for updating investigations in children's free drawing and painting.

Criteria

Rhythm and Rule

Rhythm is expressed through a flexible quality of the stroke (kinesthetically connected with a relaxed, free movement). Rhythm conveys a sensitivity to the functioning of space connected with the time element. Greek *rhy* means to "move" or to "flow"; flowing is a function of time. Such sensitivity implies elasticity and spontaneity (Fig. 7-1).

Rule is expressed through a rigid (torpid) quality of the stroke (kinesthetically connected with tight, spasmodic movements that become automatic, mechanical). Rule displays neither feeling nor connection with time. Spontaneity is lacking; planning, regulation, and rigid organization dominate (Fig. 7-2).

Rule may also be expressed through an inert (smeary and plopping) quality of the stroke (kinesthetically connected with looseness). Inertness is an escape from the spasms of rigidity, an attempt to drop out of rule, i.e., to lose control (Fig. 7-3).

Complexity and Simplicity

Complexity is expressed in a tendency toward a complete representation of the object, its individualization and differentiation. When structural, complexity is expressed through an imaginative feeling for form, a tendency toward creative form differentiation, and more intricate organization, i.e., in color, form, design, rhythm, etc. (Fig. 7-4).

Simplicity is expressed by reducing the differentiated object or structural form to the simplest pattern, that is, schematization. It conveys a loss or lack of differentiation and inability to detach the self. Simplicity also appears as conventionality (Fig. 7-5).

Expansion and Compression

Expansion is expressed by widening (opening) the space at the drawer's disposal and presenting only part of the subject. Expansion can also be seen in abstract designs that have to be completed by imagination. Expansion conveys a conscious use of space (Fig. 7-6).

Expansion may also be expressed by creating an experience of space through rhythm and integration, for example, a well-formed representation of an explosion expands the space by bursting it. Such an expression conveys controlled aggressiveness and willful and forceful activity (a rather virile form of expression). Expansion stimulates the

imagination dynamically. It conveys an atmosphere of freedom, cour-
age, adventure, and "letting go," and may be a symptom of vitality
and of a healthy, developed extraversion (Fig. 7-7).

Compression is based on a meticulous, fearful concept of space,
expressed either in the spatial appearance of the object itself or in its
spatial relationship to other objects or to the space at the drawer's
disposal. Compression conveys discomfort, a feeling of being shut in,
or of pressure and compulsion. Compression may be a symptom of
introversion or a neurosis (Figs. 7-8 and 7-9).

Integration and Disintegration

Integration is based on inner organization. It may appear as a merely
synthetic or combinative function. The feeling for the whole is notice-
able, although the expression of such feeling may be poor. Integration
may be expressed on a level comparable to that of genuine artwork.
Things (objects as well as lines and contours) are in proportion and
relationship to one another. Each element is an indispensable part of
the whole and centered around some external or internal force. Such
centrality may be expressed by representation as well as merely structurally (Fig. 7-10).

Disintegration lacks synthesis and there is no tendency toward harmony. Things (objects as well as lines and contours) are conceived in a
piecemeal way. They may be contaminated, i.e., two or more things
may be represented as one, but without relationship or coherence.
Disintegration lacks a center; nothing relates to anything else; the
product conveys coldness and alienates the viewer. Disintegration may
be a sign of eccentricity, or of personality deterioration; if connected
with other features, it can be a sign of psychosis (Fig. 7-11).

Realism and Symbolism

Realism is shown through the prevalence of representational elements and an interest in the world of objects. Structurally, realism is
expressed in a somewhat mechanical imagination, such as engineering
drawing.

Symbolism exists when the represented object obviously stands for
something else or where structure prevails throughout the drawing
(Fig. 7-12).

The relationship between one style and its opposite becomes fully
evident if one considers that a positive as well as a negative aspect can
be ascribed to each style of expression. One should appreciate the
intrinsic tension associated with each pair of opposites.

Figure 7-1. Rhythm reflects the child's inner dynamics. Age 6 years, male.

Figure 7-2. Rule reflects good control. Age 12 years, male.

Figure 7-3. Rule (inertness) reflects the static uniformity of the external world. Age 7 years, male.

Figure 7-4. Complexity reflects differentiation and totality. Age 6 years, female.

Figure 7-5. Simplicity reflects primitiveness. Age 7 years, male.

Figure 7-6. Expansion (expanding the space by bursting it). Age 8 years, male.

Theories of Autism

Figure 7-7. Expansion reflects a direction toward the surrounding world and the potential ability to make contact. Age 6 years, female.

Figure 7-8. Compression (being shut in) reflects isolation. Age 7 years, male.

Figure 7-9. Compression (compulsiveness) reflects isolation. Age 6 years, male.

Figure 7-10. Integration reflects a sense of harmony and order. Age 7 years, male. (This example was copied from *Starry Night* by van Gogh. Well-formed, fluid shapes are reflected in the clouds. The placement of the stars is well planned. If one element were removed from the picture, it would not be complete. This child integrates his ideas and information and "pushes them out" on paper.)

Figure 7-11. Disintegration reflects chaos. Age 7 years, female.

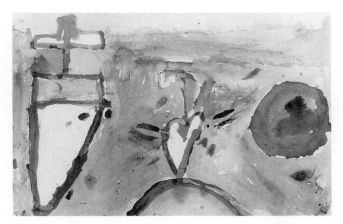

Figure 7-12. Symbolism. Age 7 years, male. (This example shows "Nuclear War"; a church and a heart represent efforts to stop the war with love.)

8

Theoretical Bases of Treatments

Speculations about the ways in which autism develops in children and the corresponding therapies vary according to the behavioral theory predominant at the time. For example, Bettelheim's therapy (1967), considered until the 1970s to be based on solid psychoanalytic theory, illustrates how theories once favored lose scientific credibility when a new step in knowledge—in this case biological knowledge—is made.

During the 1960s, when Bettelheim's therapeutic ideas prevailed, it was recommended that the autistic child be removed from parental influence and care to provide an environment totally different from the one he was presumed to have abandoned in despair. Psychoanalytic constructs placed responsibility for the autistic child's deficits directly on the parents, and they, understandably, were guilt stricken. Critics (Bender 1969; Rutter 1968) do not believe that a specific type of psychogenesis has been proved by Bettelheim's hypothesis.

PSYCHOANALYTIC THEORY

Bettelheim's Therapy

From 1956 to 1962, Bettelheim concentrated on the study and treatment of autism. His consistently held position is that to understand the individual one must first understand his or her early development and that childhood, although lost from conscious memory, persists as a significant determinant of one's life. His therapy draws from two principles: helping the child avoid everything that might reactivate thoughts of infancy and the presumed threat to his life, and encourag-

67

ing and rewarding self-initiated activity. Accordingly, in his psychoanalytic theory of autism Bettelheim attends to libidinal instincts as they come into contact with a repressive reality and adapt to its demands. The character traits of autistic children are conceptualized as symbolic derivatives of libido fixated at the oral stage of infantile psychosexual development, an outcome of inordinate frustration or lack of gratification.

The child's imagining the mother as a destructive figure, often transformed into the devouring witch of fairy tales, has, in this view, a source in reality, specifically in the mother's destructive, murderous intent. The mother, either because she is anxious or frustrated in her motherly feelings, responds to the infant with anger or injured indifference. When reality seems too destructive the child retreats, later recalling that "he was never adequately taken care of as a child" (Bettelheim 1950, p. 224).

Bettelheim's earlier task was an attempt to understand how the world could destroy the child's personality. Based on his studies of people who survived in German concentration camps and led by a belief in the power of insight and empathy, Bettelheim created a milieu that fostered reconstruction of the child's personality from what he thought to be an "ascent from hell."

Discussions of Bettelheim's theory and the resultant therapy have stirred powerful emotions and antagonisms among psychologists and therapists. The devout psychoanalyst may "throw up a wall" or defend Bettelheim's theory out of professional commitment. The modern biologist, on the other hand, may simply forge ahead, not taking time to look back and discuss the matter. The main difficulty with Bettelheim's theory is insistence on the mother's causal role. Some would argue that Bettelheim never denied that autism had an organic component, but the only support he has given that idea appears in the second half of a sentence in *The Empty Fortress* (1967). The entire sentence reads, "My own belief, as presented throughout this book, is that autism has essentially to do with everything that happens from birth on; nor can we rule out the possibility that some prenatal deviation in development may be a contributing factor" (p. 393).

As a therapist, Bettelheim has tended to empathize so completely with the autistic that he elevates the condition to heroic proportions and claims cures that are today seriously questioned. Not for his theory, but for the spirit of his therapy, for his willingness to attend to the inner life of the autistic, will Bettelheim be best remembered.

ETHOLOGICAL THEORY

E. A. and N. Tinbergen's Taming Procedure

E. A. Tinbergen and N. Tinbergen (1972, 1976) and N. Tinbergen (1974) suggested that it might be fruitful to conceptualize the phenomenology and treatment of infantile autism in terms of an ethological paradigm (Kramer and McKinney 1979). N. Tinbergen and colleagues had observed in studying the courtship behavior of gull species (1959) that courtship is organized so as to reduce the male gull's tendency to attack an approaching female and, at the same time, reduce her tendency to flee his aggressiveness. Tinbergen conceptualized this behavior as an approach-withdrawal system, with tendencies to approach and to withdraw occurring simultaneously in each of the participants. For a successful courtship, approach behavior must eventually predominate in both individuals.

Tinbergen and Tinbergen (1972) compared the social behavior of the autistic child to that of the female gull when initially approaching a male in his nesting area. In both, there is a slight tendency to approach the other individual, and a great tendency to withdraw.

Using this ethological paradigm, Tinbergen and Tinbergen hypothesize that in autistic children a wide variety of situations elicit withdrawal behavior, prompting in them an ongoing approach-withdrawal conflict. Compared with other children, withdrawal behavior in the autistic is more intense and lasting.

The Tinbergens' approach to the treatment of infantile autism is based on three postulates:

1. Autistic children have a decreased tendency to approach and an increased tendency to withdraw in social situations.
2. All of the behavior patterns seen in autistic children occur in normal children.
3. Autistic children have the capacity to engage in approach behavior patterns indistinguishable from those of normal children.

Kramer, Anderson, and Westman (1984) applied Tinbergen and Tinbergen's ethological theory to the treatment of autistic children over a five-year period. They described their activity as follows:

> The first is that within a relatively non-stimulating playroom the therapist is exceptionally careful to be non-intrusive by not looking directly at the child nor initiating touching or talking. . . .

The second activity is observing for approach behavior patterns in the child in much the same manner as an ethologist. We pay the most attention to . . . the initiation of eye contact by the child and any related changes in facial expression . . . any decrease in physical space between the child and the therapist to actual physical contact . . . the initiation of verbal interaction.

The third aspect of implementation is the response of the therapist which is in essence a mirroring of the child's approach behavior.

The fourth aspect of implementation is an extension of the third. It is the therapist's response to withdrawal and bizarre behavior on the part of the child. . . . We elected not to use Mahler's technique (1968), in which one attempts to lure the child out of the "autistic shell," feeling that it might be experienced as intrusive by the autistic child. With regard to bizarre behavior . . . we elected to look upon it as social. We therefore proceeded to mirror such behavior just as we had done with the more appropriate approach behavior patterns. . . .

The fifth aspect of this approach is the graduated nature of its use . . . an ordering of behavior from socially positive (playful interaction, touching) to socially negative (stereotypies). . . . The therapist's own behavior followed child behavior, so in one sense the scale is also a description of the psychotherapeutic technique. . . . Progress can be gauged by children spending more and more of the session in the upper portion of the scale. Although there appears to be a lag period between progress observed during the therapy session and outside the sessions, the scale provides a framework for judging overall progress as well. (pp. 107–110)

Kramer, Anderson, and Westman (1984) found that the ethological therapeutic approach offers an adjunct to a comprehensive treatment program for autistic children and merits further study. Still, the degree of nonintrusiveness suggested by Tinbergen and Tinbergen may be more than most research psychologists and therapists are willing to accept. The ethological method is one of observation in the natural setting, without in any way influencing the observed behavior. Its advantage lies in providing insight into elementary and generalizable behavioral patterns, which allows the therapist to concentrate on the social and interpersonal life of the autistic child without considering etiology.

In a series of three cases (Seifert 1990a) seen during the past 10 years, I have found, as did other researchers (Kramer and McKinney 1979; Kramer, Anderson, and Westman 1984), the Tinbergen approach to the phenomenology of infantile autism to be very helpful in conceptualizing the relationship deficit in the autistic disorder. I have also found in treating autistic children that the approach succeeds in overcoming a language gap and in establishing nonverbal communication.

ORGANIC THEORY

Biological Therapy

Attempts have recently been made to discover biochemical etiologies of autism (Ritvo et al. 1986). Biochemical abnormalities in some autistic children have been identified (Coleman 1979; Coleman and Gillberg 1985); however, no specific associations have been found. Nor has any single drug been found that helps all autistic people. Efforts to elucidate biochemical contributors to infantile autism have been confounded by the lack of diagnostic specificity and by factors such as age, sex, intellectual status, and activity level that affect the body's biochemistry.

Research interest has recently concentrated on two drugs: fenfluramine and haloperidol. Fenfluramine lowers serotonin and haloperidol blocks dopamine, both neurotransmitters in the central nervous system. Trials of the serotonin-reducing drug fenfluramine were conducted by Ritvo and colleagues (Ritvo et al. 1986) in autistic children found to have elevated concentrations of serotonin (Ritvo et al. 1970). Recent results (Ritvo et al. 1986) suggest fenfluramine may help some higher functioning autistic people by increasing their attention span and general receptivity but that it does not help the severely autistic.

A number of autistic children and adults have behavioral problems that interfere with their learning and functioning, including hyperactivity, aggressiveness, self-mutilations, stereotypic movements, temper tantrums, irritability, withdrawal or lack of interest in people, and inability to focus on a task. Currently, haloperidol is the most effective drug in reducing abnormal behaviors in autistic children (Campbell et al. 1978; Anderson et al. 1984). However, some persons who receive haloperidol or similar drugs over a prolonged period may develop side effects. Of greatest concern is that these drugs may induce abnormal involuntary movements or tardive dyskinesia.

Special precautions are required when drug therapy is prescribed to autistic persons who have an associated seizure disorder and take anti-seizure medication. Certain drugs may increase the frequency of seizures or facilitate their development—chlorpromazine is one such drug. The use of drugs, particularly in the autistic, who generally cannot communicate physical discomforts such as dry mouth, dizziness, or allergic reactions, merits careful consideration.

Naltrexone is reported to benefit a few autistic people (Campbell et al. 1988), however, additional research is required to assess its safety and efficacy with the autistic.

Certain vitamins seem to be effective in subsets of autistic children, according to studies by Rimland and colleagues (Rimland, Callaway, and Dreyfus 1978) and Martineau et al. (1988). Rimland advocates megavitamin therapy and hypothesizes that the autistic person may need more essential substances to attain normal brain functioning.

Wherever drug therapy is indicated, careful clinical and laboratory monitoring and compliance is required. Most researchers (Campbell 1988) advocate prescribing drugs only as part of a comprehensive treatment program. If an autistic child or adult displays symptoms that may be reduced by biological therapy, then the role of the drug is to make the individual more accessible to other treatment, such as special education and behavioral therapy.

LEARNING THEORY

Behavioral Therapy

Most of the treatments currently used for autism involve behavioral therapy and are directed at well-known, visible symptoms, such as severely self-injurious and assaultive behavior. Therapeutic behavioral techniques have benefited from studies of motivation and reinforcement, like those of Koegel and Mentis (1985) and Rincover and Newson (1985). Over the last 20 years behavioral therapy has become one of the major therapeutic modalities available to psychologists. Based on learning theory, it asserts that problem behaviors are involuntarily acquired and are due to inappropriate learning. Behavioral therapy concentrates on changing or modifying behavior rather than on changing unconscious or conscious thought patterns. Little attention is paid to the person himself, but a great deal of attention is given the stimuli that may elicit unwanted behavior. Specific techniques designed to facilitate behavioral changes include:

1. Operant conditioning. These techniques are based on evaluation and modification of the antecedents and consequences of a person's

behavior. Behavior is encouraged by positive reinforcement and discouraged by negative reinforcement.

2. Aversion therapy. When a person's behavior is undesirable, he is given an unpleasant stimulus, such as an electric shock or loud sound. Cessation of punishment is often associated with recovery of the original responses and recidivism rates tend to be high. This, combined with technical shortcomings and ethical objections to the inhumanity of such treatment, has limited the use of aversion therapy in clinical settings.

Common to both methods is rigorous data collection. Behavioral therapy relies on careful measurement of behavior. A technique is considered successful if it eliminates measurable undesirable behavior or increases desirable behavior. Research supports the use of both operant conditioning and aversion therapy with certain subsets of autistic individuals. (See Smith [1988] and Rimland [1988] for statements for and against aversion therapy with autistic persons.)

McGINNIS ASSOCIATION METHOD

There are still other therapies for the autistic child that do not have a developed theoretical basis. One such therapy is the association method (McGinnis 1963), which treats disordered communication in aphasic children and those with handicapping conditions that have an aphasic component such as emotional disturbance, autism, or mental retardation.

The association method was organized into a procedure shortly after World War I to teach children with a total or partial inability to understand or use language and was set forth by McGinnis in 1939. Since that time, it has been incorporated in the teaching program of the Central Institute for the Deaf in St. Louis and applied to teaching aphasic children.

The McGinnis association method develops and integrates systematically each of the specific skills of understanding and using oral communication within the essential processes of learning, i.e., attention, retention, and recall. For example, a lag in perceiving speech sounds and inability to assemble them into meaningful words and language are predominant symptoms in the condition known as sensory aphasia. Sensory aphasic children need selective listening to organize and integrate environmental language. This anomaly in perception and auditory processing can exist in intelligent aphasic children with good hearing.

The method enlists the child's close attention in pronouncing the vowels and consonants necessary to form words. The child is taught to associate the written form of the sounds with their articulation and to analyze and monitor their production. Lips and tongue movements of oral articulation are emphasized, but not exaggerated, so that a kinesthetic sense of the movement is established.

Retention and recall of sounds and words are established by attending to the written form of words, or by picture or object. In the beginning of the program, speech and language material are limited and supplemented by attention-getting activities designed to create habits of attention and exact response and to stimulate an awareness of oral communication. Progress is measured in terms of three language units.

The first language unit is devoted to teaching 50 nouns and emphasizes a simple, structured approach consisting of short, ordered steps that lead the child from simply focusing attention on the teacher to understanding and speaking the first 50 nouns on his own. The early steps in the development of oral communication include:

1. Attention-getting exercises
2. Development of single sounds
3. Combining sounds into nouns
4. Associating meaning with nouns
5. Writing readiness exercises and writing of nouns
6. Lipreading and acoustic association, first with sound elements and then with nouns
7. Association of the meaning of commands relating to daily class routine from both written and oral stimulation (McGinnis 1963, p. 62)

The second unit of language attempts to develop memory for sound sequence and introduces simple sentences, questions, descriptive stories, numbers, pronouns, prepositions, and present tense verbs by using pictures portraying activities.

The third language unit introduces more complex concepts of past tense verbs and language forms through personal experience stories that in turn prepare the child for imaginative stories. In the imaginative story the child describes not only the actions and conditions shown in a picture, but draws on his or her experiences and imagination to relate what has happened to bring about the conclusion. With the items taught in this unit, the child is better prepared to visualize described events and to understand the language used in readers and other textbooks added to their program.

McGinnis suggests that 4 years old is a good age to start the formal program, but recommends that early evaluation should not preclude reevaluation for selecting placement in a future program, since, with training, maturation may bring out attributes not observed initially.

Specifically, McGinnis (1963) views autism as a handicapping condition with an aphasic component. She suggests that social behavior sets the two defects, aphasia and autism, apart, although I believe this is an oversimplification. Nonetheless, the McGinnis association method appears promising as an adjunct to other therapies.

Notes

1. RETHINKING THEORIES OF AUTISM

1. Kanner first described the autistic syndrome in 1943, but the term did not enter the nomenclature until 1980 with publication of the *Diagnostic and Statistical Manual of Mental Disorders* (DSM-III; American Psychiatric Association). During the four intervening decades investigators reached consensus that the symptoms indicative of autism are the result of underlying neuropathology with many possible etiologies. Earlier theories of psychological causes have been discarded (Ritvo 1983).

2. A major problem confronting the field of psychology has been inconsistent use of terminology referring to the various disorders included under the general designation "early childhood psychosis" (e.g., infantile autism, childhood schizophrenia, early childhood schizophrenia, early infantile psychosis, and symbiotic psychosis). The term "early childhood psychosis" is no longer considered useful by most researchers and clinicians, since it may mislead one into assuming an association between this condition and adult psychotic disorders, a possibility that appears more and more remote. Reflecting this attitude is the DSM-III-R (American Psychiatric Association 1987), which uses the term "pervasive developmental disorder" and includes infantile autism as one category under this general classification. Childhood schizophrenia, on the other hand, is classified in DSM-III-R under the same subcategories as adult schizophrenias.

3. Campbell's *Psychiatric Dictionary* (1981), defines affect as "The feeling-tone accompaniment of an idea or mental representation. . . . The term affect is also used, more loosely, as a class name for feeling, emotion, or *mood*" (p. 15). The astute reader will note that in this definition of affect, the word "idea" implies cognition and that affect is an integral part of intelligence. For purposes of this study, affect will be discussed in the light of cognitive development and will be assumed to have a physiological origin influenced by environment and controlled by cognition. Affect is peculiar to humanness, and its study is rooted in the study of human nature.

2. DEFINING AUTISM

1. Used with permission from "Early Childhood Autism: An Ethological Approach" by E. A. Tinbergen and N. Tinbergen, 1972, *Beihefte zur Zeitschrift für Tierpsychologie,* 10, pp. 1–53. See N. Tinbergen and E. A. Tinbergen's (1983) new formulation of their 1972 work, *Autistic Chil-*

dren: New Hope for a Cure. In some respects it is a reversal of their earlier work and expresses an opposite position toward therapy.

3. AN EVOLUTIONARY VIEW OF PERSONALITY DEVELOPMENT

1. Holism is an approach to the study of behavior that insists that all behavior be considered in its full biological context (Goldstein 1939).
2. The great brain gap between man and other animals can be visualized by observing what happens when a man's hand prods the outspread tentacles of a sea anemone. The anemone will instantly retract its tentacles into its body; the reaction is automatic, since what passes for a brain in the anemone is programmed for only one pattern of action: in response to touch the tentacle retracts. No reasoned behavior is involved. But the man may pull his hand back, or he may not. His brain considers options, and his action will depend on many things—whether he thinks anemones are dangerous or harmless, whether the contact is pleasing or discomforting, whether he touched the anemone on purpose or accidentally. *Life Before Man,* p. 19 (New York: Time-Life Books, 1972).
3. Phenocopy is an environmentally produced change in phenotype that mimics a trait known to be caused by a genetic change.
4. I saw affect expressed by the sexes in the human-figure drawings of 4- to 5-year-old, 8- ·to 9-year-old, and 13- to 14-year-old Chinese and Afro-American children. (See *Holistic Interpretation of Autism: A Theoretical Framework* [Seifert 1990b] for detailed findings.) Some striking parallels in cross-culturally consistent sex differences may reflect psychobiological differences.

    An analysis of 260 human-figure drawings from Chinese and Afro-American groups showed certain consistencies. In a broad comparison of human-figure drawings by boys and girls, boys in both cultures drew more male figures and girls more female figures. Girls at all ages more often included flowers. Boys, ages 4–5, also included flowers, although unlike the girls, flower-drawing boys also included moving vehicles such as cars, rockets, and trucks. Boys, ages 8–9 and 13–14, in both cultural groups exhibited more movement and aggression in their drawings compared with girls, who exhibited more passivity.

    In addition to cross-cultural sex differences, there were cultural differences between the sexes in the way affect was expressed. The drawings of Chinese boys, 8 to 9, and 13 to 14 years old, exhibited virility in controlled ways and showed aggression in a more symbolic fashion—for instance, incorporating competitiveness in mythical figures and in kings with crowns. Unlike the Chinese boys, 8- to 9- and 13- to 14-year-old Afro-American boys assumed the hero's role in their drawings as musclemen and as killers and gangsters with guns and knives. Chinese girls, 8 to

9 and 13 to 14 years old, exhibited femaleness in physically attrac-
tive, princesslike figure drawings, expressed in comely, controlled ways.
Afro-American girls, 8 to 9 and 13 to 14 years old, exhibited femaleness in
highly sexualized figures, with accentuated eyelashes and lips, shapely
bodies, and "bustiness."

One other finding emerges from this study. As a group, Chinese children, 4 to 5, 8 to 9, and 13 to 14 years old, exhibited in their drawings a
placid, accommodating attitude. Emotional expression was consistently
highly controlled, conveying a sense of restraint or impassivity. The same
age Afro-Americans exhibited strong affect and extremes in affect. Chinese children behaved thoughtfully and studiously as a group, while Afro-
American children impulsively acted out their feelings.

The drawings are included as a cross-cultural approach to the question
of innate sex differences in affectivity. I concluded that there are cross-
culturally consistent sex differences in human-figure drawing that may
reflect psychobiological differences. This finding may support a psychobiological approach to the question of affectlessness in autism, and the affective differences in autistic children may be attributable to constitutional
differences. (See Seifert [1988a, 1988b, 1990a, 1990b] for the study of
human-figure drawings by autistic children.)

5. Actualization is used in Goldstein's (1939) sense: there is only one drive
   that is invariant and characteristic of all living organisms, the drive to
   actualize inborn capacities. All other so-called drives are variable and
   subsidiary.

4. PIAGET'S ANALYSIS OF INTELLIGENCE

1. Smiling in an infant can be evoked by a definite stimulus configuration;
   modifying that stimulus configuration will fail to evoke the smile, which
   suggests that smiling is an inborn mechanism, like a reflex.

   The infant smiles at objects as well as at people. The smile, in fact,
   occurs to some extent in all general activities of adequacy; thus not all
   infant smiling is true smiling.

   The earliest nonelicited infant smiling occurs, for example, after feeding and as the infant falls asleep. This appears in the first few weeks of life
   and by the end of the first month may be evoked by touching parts of the
   face and especially the lips (Laroche and Tcheng 1963), by certain auditory stimuli, or by the gestalt of the human face and eyes (Kaila 1932).
   During about the third month, smiling becomes less stimulus-bound; the
   infant then begins to smile more selectively. In the third quarter of the first
   year, the infant responds to certain familiar people and not to unfamiliar
   ones.

   Freedman (1961) pointed out that, since human infants do not cling as do other primates, vision is the major mode of contact in the first half year, and the smile is the major means by which parent-child rapport is established.

In the autistic child the social smiling that serves to facilitate attachment and other interactions is initially missing; this lack, plus the problem of affect, may become part of a complex negative feedback circuit in the autistic child (Goldstein 1959). The autistic child seems to be arrested at the first stage of the attachment process, rather than moving on to social attachments.

2. 1880–1968. Note that Keller had sight and hearing until 18 months, at which time she contracted meningitis and lost both senses.

7. HUMAN-FIGURE DRAWING AS A PROJECTION OF AUTISTIC EXPERIENCE

1. *Kopffüsser* is a rendering of the human body as head and legs, with arms protruding from the head (*bonhomme têtard* of Luquet [1913, 1920] or "tadpole" of the English writers).

References

Alexander, F. M. 1932. *The Use of Self.* London: Chaterston.

Alschuler, R., and Hattwick, L. W. 1947. *Painting and Personality.* Chicago: University of Chicago Press.

American Psychiatric Association. 1980. *Diagnostic and Statistical Manual of Mental Disorders.* 3rd ed. Washington: American Psychiatric Association.

———. 1987. *Diagnostic and Statistical Manual of Mental Disorders.* 3rd ed. revised. Washington: American Psychiatric Association.

Anderson, L. T., Campbell, M., Grega, D. M., Perry, R., Small, A. M., and Green, W. H. 1984. Haloperidol in the treatment of infantile autism: effects on learning and behavioral symptoms. *American Journal of Psychiatry* 141(10):1195–202.

Bender, L. 1937. Art and therapy on the mental disturbances of children. *Journal of Nervous and Mental Disease* 86:249–63.

———. 1938. *A Visual Motor Gestalt Test and Its Clinical Use.* American Orthopsychiatric Association Research Monograph 3.

———. 1947. Childhood schizophrenia. *American Journal of Orthopsychiatry* 17:40–56.

———. 1949. Psychological principles of the visual motor gestalt test. Series II. *Transactions of the New York Academy of Sciences* 2(5):164–70.

———. 1960. Autism in children with mental deficiency. *American Journal of Mental Deficiency* 64:81–86.

———. 1969. A longitudinal study of schizophrenic children with autism. *Hospital and Community Psychiatry* 20:230–37.

———. 1973. The life course of children with schizophrenia. *American Journal of Psychiatry* 130:783–86.

Bender, L., and Rapaport, J. 1944. Animal drawings of children. *American Journal of Orthopsychiatry* 14:521–27.

Bender, L., and Woltmann, A. 1937. The use of plastic material as a psychiatric approach to the emotional problems of children. *American Journal of Orthopsychiatry* 7:283–300.

Benson, D. F. 1979. *Aphasia, Alexia, and Agraphia.* New York: Churchill Livingstone.

Bettelheim, B. 1950. *Love Is Not Enough: The Treatment of Emotionally Disturbed Children.* New York: Free Press.

———. 1967. *The Empty Fortress: Infantile Autism and the Birth of the Self.* New York: Free Press.

———. 1974. *A Home for the Heart.* New York: Knopf.

Blank, M., and Bridger, W. H. 1966. Conceptual cross-modal transfer in deaf and hearing children. *Child Development* 37:29–38.

Borelli, M. 1951. La naissance des opérations logiques chez des sourdmuets [The beginning of logical operations in deaf-mutes]. *Enfance* (1951, article no. 4), 222–38.

Bowlby, J. 1958. The nature of the child's tie to his mother. *International Journal of Psychoanalysis* 30:350–73.

Brazelton, T. B., and Freedman, D. G. 1971. Manual to accompany Cambridge newborn behavioral and neurological scales. In *Normal and Abnormal Development of Brain and Behaviour*, edited by G. B. A. Stoelinga and J. J. van der Werff ten Bosch, pp. 104–32. Leiden: Leiden University Press.

Buck, J. 1948. The house-tree-person technique: a qualitative and quantitative scoring manual. *Journal of Clinical Psychology* 4:317–96.

Campbell, M. 1988. Ask the experts. Dr. Magda Campbell on medications. *Advocate* 20(4):7–8, 16.

Campbell, M., Adams, P., Small, A. M., Tesch, L. M., and Curren, E. L. 1988. Naltrexone in infantile autism. *Psychopharmacology Bulletin* 24(1):135–39.

Campbell, M., Anderson, L. T., Meier, M., Cohen, I. L., Small, A. M., Samit, C., and Sachar, E. J. 1978. A comparison of haloperidol, behavior therapy and their interaction in autistic children. *Journal of the American Academy of Child Psychiatry* 17:640–55.

Campbell, R. J. 1981. *Psychiatric Dictionary*. 5th ed. New York: Oxford University Press.

Cantor, G. N. 1955. Effects of three types of pretraining on discrimination learning in preschool children. *Journal of Experimental Psychology* 49:339–42.

Cantwell, D. P., Baker, L., and Rutter, M. 1979. Families of autistic and dysphasic children. *Archives of General Psychiatry* 36:682–87.

Chess, S. 1971. Autism in children with congenital rubella. *Journal of Autism and Childhood Schizophrenia* 1:33–47.

————. 1977. Follow-up report on autism in congenital rubella. *Journal of Autism and Childhood Schizophrenia* 7:68–81.

Clancy, H., and McBride, G. 1969. The autistic process and its treatment. *Journal of Child Psychology and Psychiatry, and Applied Disciplines* 10:233–44.

Coleman, M. 1979. Studies of the autistic syndromes. In *Congenital and Acquired Cognitive Disorders*, edited by R. Katzman. *The Association for Research in Nervous and Mental Disease* 57:265–75.

Coleman, M., and Gillberg, C. 1985. *The Biology of the Autistic Syndromes*. New York: Praeger.

Courchesne, Eric. November 1988. Telephone conversation with author.

Courchesne, E., Yeung-Courchesne, R., Press, G. A., Hesselink, J. R., and Jernigan, T. L. 1988. Hypoplasia of cerebellar vermal lobules VI and VII in autism. *New England Journal of Medicine* 318:1349–54.

Cox, A., Rutter, M., Newman, S., and Bartak, L. 1975. A comparative study of infantile autism and specific developmental receptive language disorder. II. Parental characteristics. *British Journal of Psychiatry* 126:146–59.

DeMyer, M. K. 1979. *Parents and Children in Autism*. Washington: Winston.

DeMyer, M. K., Barton, S., and Norton, J. A. 1972. A comparison of adaptive, verbal, and motor profiles of psychotic and non-psychotic subnormal children. *Journal of Autism and Childhood Schizophrenia* 2:359–77.

DeMyer, M. K., Hingtgen, J. N., and Jackson, R. K. 1981. Infantile autism reviewed: a decade of research. *Schizophrenia Bulletin* 7:388–451.

Despert, J. L. 1937*a*. Technical approaches used in the study and treatment of emotional problems in children. II. Using a knife under certain definite conditions. *Psychiatric Quarterly* 11(1):111–30.

———. 1937*b*. Technical approaches used in the study and treatment of emotional problems in children. III. Drawing. *Psychiatric Quarterly* 11 (1):267–95.

———. 1938. *Emotional Problems in Children*. New York: State Hospital Press.

Dobzhansky, T. 1937. *Genetics and the Origin of Species*. New York: Columbia University Press.

Elkisch, P. 1945. Children's drawings in a projective technique. *Psychological Monographs* 58(1):1–31.

Elliott, D. E., and Needleman, R. M. 1976. The syndrome of hyperlexia. *Brain and Language* 3:339–49.

Erlenmeyer-Kimling, L., and Jarvik, L. F. 1963. Genetics and intelligence: a review. *Science* 142:1477–79.

Folstein, S., and Rutter, M. 1977*a*. Infantile autism: a genetic study of 21 twin pairs. *Journal of Child Psychology and Psychiatry* 18:297–321.

———. 1977*b*. Genetic influences and infantile autism. *Nature* 265:726–28.

Freedman, D. G. 1958. Constitutional and environmental interaction in rearing four breeds of dogs. *Science* 127:585–86.

———. 1961. The infant's fear of strangers and the flight response. *Journal of Child Psychology and Psychiatry* 4:242–48.

———. 1963. *Development of the Smile and Fear of Strangers, with an Inquiry into Inheritance of Behavior*. Film. University of Pennsylvania: Psychological Cinema Register, PCR-2140.

———. 1964. Smiling in blind infants and the issue of innate versus acquired. *Journal of Child Psychology and Psychiatry* 5:171–84.

———. 1965*a*. An ethological approach to the genetical study of human behavior. In *Methods and Goals in Human Behavior Genetics,* edited by S. Vandenberg, pp. 141–61. New York: Academic Press.

———. 1965*b*. Hereditary control of early social behavior. In *Determinants of Infant Behaviour III,* edited by B. M. Foss, pp. 149–59. London: Methuen.

———. 1967. A biological view of man's social behavior. In *Social Behavior from Fish to Man,* edited by W. Etkin, pp. 152–88. Chicago: University of Chicago Press.

———. 1968*a*. An evolutionary framework for behavioral research. In *Progress in Human Behavior Genetics,* edited by S. G. Vandenberg, pp. 1–5. Baltimore: Johns Hopkins Press.

———. 1968*b*. Personality development in infancy: a biological approach. In *Perspectives in Human Evolution,* edited by S. Washburn, vol. 1, pp. 258–87. New York: Holt, Rinehart & Winston.

———. 1971*a*. The impact of behavior genetics and ethology. In *Perspectives in Child Psychopathology,* edited by H. E. Rie, pp. 219–66. Chicago: Aldine-Atherton.

———. 1971*b*. Genetic influences on development of behavior. In *Normal and Abnormal Development of Brain and Behaviour,* edited by G. B. A. Stoelinga and J. J. van der Werff ten Bosch, pp. 208–33. Leiden: Leiden University Press.

———. 1971*c*. An evolutionary approach to research on the life cycle. *Human Development* 14:87–99.

———. 1971*d*. Behavioral assessment in infancy. In *Normal and Abnormal Development of Brain and Behavior,* edited by G. B. A. Stoelinga and J. J. van der Werff ten Bosch, pp. 92–99. Leiden: Leiden University Press.

———. 1974. *Human Infancy: An Evolutionary Perspective.* New York: Wiley.

———. 1975*a*. The origins of social behaviour. In *Influences on Human Development,* 2nd ed., edited by M. A. Mahoney, pp. 43–47. Hinsdale, Ill.: Dryden Press. (Reprinted from *Science Journal* 3 [1967]:69–73.)

———. 1975*b*. The development of social hierarchies. In *Society, Stress and Disease.* Vol. 2, *Childhood and Adolescence,* edited by L. Levi, pp. 36–42. London: Oxford University Press.

———. 1976. Infancy, biology, and culture. In *Developmental Psychobiology,* edited by L. R. Lipsitt, pp. 35–54. Hillsdale, N.J.: Erlbaum.

———. 1979. *Human Sociobiology.* New York: Free Press.

Freedman, D. G., and Freedman, N. 1969. Behavioural differences between Chinese-American and European-American newborns. *Nature* 224:1227.

Freedman, D. G., and Keller, B. 1963. Inheritance of behavior in infants. *Science* 140:196–98.

Freedman, D. G., King, J. A., and Elliot, O. 1961. Critical period in the social development of dogs. *Science* 133:1016–17.

Freedman, D. G., Loring, C. B., and Martin, R. M. 1967. Emotional behavior and personality development. In *Infancy and Early Childhood: A Handbook and Guide to Human Development,* edited by Y. Brackbill, pp. 429–502. New York: Free Press.

Freedman, D. G., and Omark, D. R. 1973. Ethology, genetics, and education. In *Cultural Relevance and Educational Issues,* edited by F. A. J. Ianni and E. Storey, pp. 249–83. Boston: Little, Brown.

Furth, H. G. 1961. The influence of language on the development of concept formation in deaf children. *Journal of Abnormal Psychology and Social Psychology* 63:386–89.

———. 1964. Research with the deaf: implications for language and cognition. *Psychological Bulletin* 62(3):145–64.

Geschwind, N., Quadfasel, F. A., and Segarra, J. 1968. Isolation of the speech area. *Neuropsychologia* 6:327–40.

Gesell, A., and Amatruda, C. S. 1948. *Developmental Diagnosis.* New York: Hoeber.

Goldfarb, W., Spitzer, R. L., and Endicott, J. A. 1976. A study of psychopathology of parents and psychotic children by structured interview. *Journal of Autism and Childhood Schizophrenia* 6:327–38.

Goldstein, K. 1939. *The Organism.* New York: American Books.

———. 1948. *Language and Language Disturbances.* New York: Grune & Stratton.

———. 1959. Abnormal conditions in infancy. *Journal of Nervous and Mental Disease* 128:538–57.

Goldstein, K., and Scheerer, M. 1941. Abstract and concrete behavior: an experimental study with special tests. *Psychological Monographs* 53:1–151.

Goodenough, F. L. 1926. *Measurement of Intelligence by Drawings.* Yonkers, N.Y.: World Book Co.

Gottesman, I. I., and Shields, J. 1967. A polygenic theory of schizophrenia. *Proceedings of the National Academy of Science* 58:199–205.

Hathaway, S. R., and McKinley, J. C. 1943–67. *Minnesota Multiphasic Personality Inventory.* Minn.: University of Minnesota Press.

Hauser, S. L., DeLong, G. R., and Rosman, N. P. 1975. Pneumographic findings in the infantile autism syndrome: a correlation with temporal lobe disease. *Brain* 98:667–88.

Heilman, K. M., Tucker, D. M., and Valenstein, E. 1976. A case of mixed transcortical aphasia with intact naming. *Brain* 99:415–26.

Höfler, R. 1927. Ueber die Bedeutung der Abstraktion für die geistige Entwicklung des taubstummen Kindes [About the sense (meaning) of abstraction for the mental development of deaf children]. *Zeitschrift für Kinderforschung* 33:414–44.

Hutt, C. 1972. *Males and Females.* Baltimore: Penguin.

Hutt, S. J., and Hutt, C. 1970. *Direct Observation and Measurement of Behaviour*. Springfield, Ill.: Thomas.

Huttenlocher, P. R., and Huttenlocher, J. 1973. A study of children with hyperlexia. *Neurology* 23:1107–16.

Huxley, J. 1943. *Evolution: The Modern Synthesis*. New York: Harper.

Itard, J. M. G. [1801, 07] 1932, 62. *L'enfant sauvage* [*The Wild Boy of Aveyron*]. Translated by G. Humphrey and M. Humphrey. New York: Appleton-Century-Crofts. (Original two reports published in 1801 and 1807; original work published in 1932.)

Jolly, C. J. 1970. The seed-eaters: a new model of hominid differentiation based on a baboon analogy. *Man* 5:5–26.

Kaila, E. 1932. Die Reaktionen des Säuglings auf das menschliche Gesicht [The reactions of the infant to the human face]. *Annales Universitatis Aboensis*, B ser., 17:1–114.

Kanner, L. 1943. Autistic disturbances of affective contact. *Nervous Child* 2:217–50.

———. 1949. Problems of nosology and psychodynamics of early infantile autism. *American Journal of Orthopsychiatry* 19:416–26.

———. 1969. "Speech on acceptance of citation delivered at annual meeting of the National Society for Autistic Children," 17–19 July, in Washington, D.C.

Kellogg, R. 1970. *Analyzing Children's Art*. Palo Alto, Calif.: Mayfield Publishing.

Kellogg, R., and O'Dell, S. 1967. *The Psychology of Children's Art*. Del Mar, Calif.: CRM Random House.

Klages, L. 1923. *Ausdrucksbewegung und Gestaltungskraft* [*Gesture and Creation*], 3rd and 4th ed. Leipzig: Barth.

Koegel, R. L., and Mentis, M. 1985. Motivation in children with autism: can they or won't they? *Journal of Child Psychology and Psychiatry, and Allied Disciplines* 26(2):185–91.

Koppitz, E. M. 1968. *Psychological Evaluation of Children's Human Figure Drawings*. New York: Grune & Stratton.

Kramer, D. A., Anderson, R. B., and Westman, J. C. 1984. The corrective autistic experience: an application of the models of Tinbergen and Mahler. *Child Psychiatry and Human Development* 15:104–20.

Kramer, D. A., and McKinney, W. T. Jr. 1979. The overlapping territories of psychiatry and ethology. *Journal of Nervous and Mental Disease* 167(1):3–22.

Krautter, O. 1930. Die Entwicklung des plastischen Gestaltens beim vorschulpflichtigen Kinde. Ein Beitrag zur Psychogenese der Gestaltung [Formation of plastic forms by preschool children. More about the psychogenesis of forms]. *Beiheft 15 zur Zeitschrift für angewandte Psychologie*. Leipzig: Barth.

Laroche, J. L., and Tcheng, F. 1963. *Le sourire du nourisson: La voix comme facteur declenchant [The Smile of the Nursling: The Voice as a Releasing Factor]*, pp. 7–8. Louvain Université de Louvain.

Lotter, V. 1966. Epidemiology of autistic conditions in young children: I. prevalence. *Social Psychiatry* 1:124–37.

Lowenfeld, V. 1954. *Your Child and His Art*. New York: Macmillan.

Luquet, H. G. 1913. *Les dessins d'un enfant: Etude psychologique [The Drawings of a Child: Psychological Study]*. Paris: Alcan.

———. 1920. Les bonhommes têtards dans le dessin enfantin [Tadpole figures in juvenile drawing]. *Journal de Psychologie Normale et Pathologique* 17:684–710.

———. 1927. *Le dessin enfantin [Juvenile Drawing]*. Paris: Alcan.

Luria, A. R. 1961. *The Role of Speech in the Regulation of Normal and Abnormal Behavior*. New York: Liveright.

McAdoo, W. G., and DeMyer, M. K. 1978a. Personality characteristics of parents. In *Autism: A Reappraisal of Concepts and Treatment*, edited by M. Rutter and E. Schopler, pp. 251–67. New York: Plenum.

———. 1978b. Research related to family factors in autism. *Journal of Pediatric Psychology* 2:162–66.

MacAndrew, H. 1948. Rigidity and isolation: a study of the deaf and the blind. *Journal of Abnormal Psychology and Social Psychology* 43:476–94.

McGinnis, M. A. 1963. *Aphasic Children*. Washington, D.C.: Alexander Graham Bell Association for the Deaf.

Machover, K. 1949. *Personality Projection in the Drawing of the Human Figure*. Springfield, Ill.: Thomas.

Mahler, M. S. 1968. *On Human Symbiosis and the Vicissitudes of Individuation*. Vol. 1. New York: International Universities Press.

Martineau, J., Barthelemy, C., Cheliakine, C., and Lelord, G. 1988. Brief report: an open middle-term study of combined vitamin B6-magnesium in a subgroup of autistic children selected for their sensitivity to this treatment. *Journal of Autism and Developmental Disorders* 18(3):435–47.

Massie, H. N. 1978. Blind ratings of mother-infant interaction in home movies of pre-psychotic and normal infants. *American Journal of Psychiatry* 135:1371–74.

Mayr, E. 1958. Behavior and systematics. In *Behavior and Evolution*, edited by A. Roe and G. G. Simpson, pp. 341–62. New Haven: Yale University Press.

Mendel, G. J. [1865] 1960. *Experiments in Plant Hybridization*. Cambridge: Harvard University Press. (Original work published in 1865 as *Versuch über pflanzen-hybriden* in the Proceedings of the Brünn Natural History Society, Verh. Natur. Ver. Brünn 4.)

Montague, J. A. 1951. Spontaneous drawings of the human form in childhood schizophrenia. In *An Introduction to Projective Techniques*, edited by H. H. Anderson and G. L. Anderson, pp. 370–85. New York: Prentice-Hall.

Myklebust, H. R. 1978. Toward a science of dyslexiology. In *Progress in Learning Disabilities,* edited by H. R. Myklebust, vol. 4, pp. 1–39. New York: Grune & Stratton.

Myklebust, H. R., Killen, J., and Bannochie, M. 1972. Emotional characteristics of learning disability. *Journal of Autism and Childhood Schizophrenia* 2:151–59.

Newman, H. H., Freeman, F. N., and Holzinger, K. J. 1937. *Twins: A Study of Heredity and Environment.* Chicago: University of Chicago Press.

O'Connor, N., and Hermelin, B. 1959. Discrimination and reversal learning in imbeciles. *Journal of Abnormal and Social Psychology* 59:409–13.

Ogden, C. K., and Richards, I. A. 1967. Thoughts, words and things. In *The Psychology of Language, Thought and Instruction,* edited by J. P. De-Cecco, pp. 140–47. New York: Holt, Rinehart & Winston.

O'Gorman, G. 1970. *The Nature of Childhood Autism.* London: Butterworths.

Oléron, P. 1953. Conceptual thinking of the deaf. *American Annals of the Deaf* 98:304–10.

Phyles, M. K. 1932. Verbalization as a factor in learning. *Child Development* 3:108–13.

Piaget, J. [1947] 1950. *The Psychology of Intelligence.* Translated by M. Percy and D. E. Berlyne. London: Routledge & Kegan Paul. (Original work published in 1947 as *La psychologie de l'intelligence.* A. Colin, Paris.)

———. [1936] 1952. *The Origins of Intelligence in Children.* Translated by M. Cook. New York: International Universities Press. (Original work published in 1936 as *La naissance de l'intelligence chez l'enfant.* Delachaux & Niestlé, Neuchâtel.)

———. [1937] 1954. *The Construction of Reality in the Child.* Translated by M. Cook. New York: Basic Books. (Original work published in 1937 as *La construction du reél chez l'enfant.* Delachaux & Niestlé, Neuchâtel.)

Piaget, J., and Inhelder, B. [1966] 1969. *The Psychology of the Child.* Translated by H. Weaver. New York: Basic Books. (Original work published in 1966 as *La psychologie de l'enfant.* Presses Universitaires de France, Paris.)

Potts, D. M. 1970. Which is the weaker sex? *Journal of Biosocial Science* 2 (Suppl.):147–57.

Prinzhorn, H. 1923. *Bildnerei der Geisteskranken: Ein Beitrag zur Psychologie und Psychopathologie der Gestaltung* [*Drawing of the Mentally Ill: On the Psychology and Psychopathology of Design*], 2nd ed. Berlin: Verlag Julius Springer.

Prior, M. R., and Bradshaw, J. L. 1979. Hemisphere functioning in autistic children. *Cortex* 15:73–81.

Rimland, B. 1964. *Infantile Autism: The Syndrome and Its Implications for a Neural Theory of Behavior*. Englewood Cliffs, N.J.: Prentice-Hall.

———. 1988. ASA resolution on aversives: statements for and against. *Advocate* 20(4):10–14.

Rimland, B., Callaway, E., and Dreyfus, P. 1978. The effects of high doses of vitamin B_6 on autistic children: a double blind cross-over study. *American Journal of Psychiatry* 135(4):472–75.

Rincover, A., and Newson, C. D. 1985. The relative motivational properties of sensory and edible reinforcers in teaching autistic children. *Journal of Applied Behavior Analysis* 18(3):237–48.

Ritvo, E. R. 1981. Genetic and immuno-hematological studies on the syndrome of autism. *Proceedings of the 1981 International Conference on Autism*, pp. 171–76. Washington: National Society for Children and Adults with Autism.

———. 1983. The syndrome of autism: a medical model. *Integrative Psychiatry* 1:103–22.

———. 1985. "Genetic Studies of Autism." Speech presented at the National Society for Children and Adults with Autism annual meeting, Los Angeles, 10–13 July 1985.

Ritvo, E. R., Freeman, B. J., Mason-Brothers, A., Mo, A., and Ritvo, A. M. 1985. Concordance for the syndrome of autism in 40 pairs of afflicted twins. *American Journal of Psychiatry* 142:74–77.

Ritvo, E. R., Freeman, B. J., Yuwiler, A., Geller, E., Schroth, P., Yokota, A., Mason-Brothers, A., August, G. J., Klykylo, W., Leventhal, B. L., Lewis, K., Piggott, L. E., Realmuto, G., Stubbs, E. G., and Umansky, R. 1986. Fenfluramine treatment of autism: UCLA-collaborative study of 81 patients at 9 medical centers. *Psychopharmacology Bulletin* 22(1):133–40.

Ritvo, E. R., Spence, M. A., Freeman, B. J., Mason-Brothers, A., and Marazita, M. L. 1985. Evidence for autosomal recessive inheritance in 46 families with multiple incidence of autism. *American Journal of Psychiatry* 142:187–92.

Ritvo, E. R., Yuwiler, A., Geller, E., Ornitz, E. M., Saeger, K., Plotkin, S. 1970. Increased blood serotonin and platelets in early infantile autism. *Archives of General Psychiatry* 23:566–72.

Rorschach, H. [1921] 1969. *Psychodiagnostics*. Translated by P. Lemkau and B. Kronenberg, 7th ed. New York: Grune & Stratton. (Original work published in 1921 as *Psychodiagnostik: Methodik und Ergebnisse eines Wahrnehmungsdiagnostischen Experiments*. Verlag Hans Huber, Bern, Medical Publisher. Printed in Switzerland [Renewed 1948].)

Rutter, M. 1967. Psychotic disorders in early childhood. In *Recent Develop-*

ments in Schizophrenia: A Symposium, edited by A. Coppen and A. Walk. *British Journal of Psychiatry* 1:133–58.

———. 1968. Concepts of autism. *Journal of Child Psychology and Psychiatry* 9:1–25.

———. 1974. The development of infantile autism. *Psychological Medicine* 4:147–63.

———. 1978. Diagnosis and definition of childhood autism. *Journal of Autism and Childhood Schizophrenia* 8:139–61.

Schopler, E. 1974. The stress of autism as ethology. *Journal of Autism and Childhood Schizophrenia* 4(3):193–96.

Seifert, C. D. 1988*a*. The human-figure drawing in the treatment of an autistic adolescent. *Child Psychiatry and Human Development* 19(1):74–81.

———. 1988*b*. Learning from drawings: an autistic child looks out at us. *The American Journal of Art Therapy* 27(2):45–53.

———. 1990*a*. *Case Studies in Autism: A Young Child and Two Adolescents.* Lanham, Md.: University Press of America.

———. 1990*b*. *Holistic Interpretation of Autism: A Theoretical Framework.* Lanham, Md.: University Press of America.

Siegel, I. E. 1953. Developmental trends in the abstraction ability of children. *Child Development* 24:131–44.

Smith, M. D. 1988. ASA resolution on aversives: statements for and against. *Advocate* 20(4):10–14.

Thompson, J. 1941. The ability of children of different grade levels to generalize on sorting tasks. *Journal of Psychology* 11:119–26.

Thompson, J. S., and Thompson, M. W. 1986. *Genetics in Medicine.* 4th ed. Philadelphia: W. B. Saunders.

Time-Life Books. 1972. *Life Before Man.* New York: Time-Life Books.

Tinbergen, E. A., and Tinbergen, N. 1972. Early childhood autism: an ethological approach. *Beihefte zur Zeitschrift für Tierpsychologie* 10:1–53.

———. 1976. The aetiology of childhood autism: a criticism of the Tinbergens' theory: a rejoinder. *Psychological Medicine* 6:545–49.

Tinbergen, N. 1959. Comparative studies of the behaviour of gulls (Laridae): a progress report. *Behaviour* 15:1–70.

———. 1964. Aggression and fear in the normal behaviour of some animals. In *The Pathology and Treatment of Sexual Deviation,* edited by I. Rosen, pp. 3–23. Oxford: Oxford University Press.

———. 1974. Ethology and stress diseases. *Science* 185:20–23.

Tinbergen, N., and Tinbergen, E. A. 1983. *Autistic Children: New Hope for a Cure.* Winchester: Allen & Unwin.

Treffert, D. A. 1970. Epidemiology of infantile autism. *Archives of General Psychiatry* 22:431–38.

Troup, E. 1938. A comparative study by means of the Rorschach method of personality development in twenty pairs of identical twins. *Genetic Psychology Monographs* 20:461–556.

Vandenberg, S. G. 1966. *Hereditary Factors in Normal Personality Traits.* Louisville: University of Louisville, Department of Pediatrics, Twin Study Child Development Unit.

Vincent, M. 1956. Rôle des données perceptives dans l'abstraction [The role of perceptual givens in abstract cognition]. *Enfance* (1956, article no. 4), 1–20.

Weigl, E. 1941. On the psychology of so-called processes of abstraction. *Journal of Abnormal and Social Psychology* 36:3–33.

Wing, L. 1970. The syndrome of early childhood autism. *British Journal of Hospital Medicine* 1970 (September):381–92.

———. 1979. The current status of childhood autism. *Psychological Medicine* 9:9–12.

Wing, L., and Ricks, D. M. 1976. The aetiology of childhood autism: a criticism of the Tinbergens' ethological theory. *Psychological Medicine* 6:533–43.

Index

Abstract thought, 23, 39
  see also Conceptualization; Semiotic function
Actualization, 33
  defined, 79n.
Affect, 5, 35, 80n.
  aphasia and, 54
  defined, 77n.
  in human figure drawing, 3, 78–79n.
  problems of, treatment in, 15
Affective imbalance, 7
Alexander, F. M., 14
Alschuler, R., 57
Amatruda, C. S., 57
Anderson, L. T., 71
Anderson, R. B., 15, 69–70
Anxiety, 7
  see also Fear
Aphasia
  autism and, 51–54
  central, 51, 54
  expressive, 51
  mixed transcortical aphasia syndrome, 52–53
  receptive, 51
  sensory, 73
  treatment with association method, 73–75
Apprehension, 7
  in child-stranger encounters, 11
  see also Fear
Approach-withdrawal, 13, 69
  see also Child-stranger encounters; Motivational conflict; Withdrawal
Association method, 73–75
Attachment formations, 18, 80n.
Autism
  aphasia and, 51–54
  behavioral therapy, 72–73
  Bettelheim on, 1–2, 26, 67–68
  biological treatment, 71–72
  brain injury or abnormality and, 5, 24–25, 50
  central nervous system damage and, 5, 28
  cognitive development and, 35–42
  communicative pathology and, 5, 6;
    see also Language
  defined, 5–6, 77n., 78n.
  degrees of, 6
  developmental theories and, 35–42, 47–48
  drawing, or human figure drawing and, 2–3, 39–40, 55–66, 79n.

ethological approach to, 7–16, 69–71
gender and, 29, 32
genetic factors and, 24–33
incidence of, 6, 29
I.Q. and, 5–6, 29
language and, 40–42, 43–50
McGinnis association method, 73–75
-normal continuum, 8, 9, 10, 11, 12
parents and, 26–28
as psychosis, 1–2, 77n.
semiotic function and, 39–41
smiling and, 80n.; *see also* Child-stranger encounters
social pathology and, 5, 6, 7–16, 40–41
symptomatology of, 6–7
thought and, 43–50
treatment, or therapy, 14–16, 29–31, 56, 67–75
twins in studies of, 24–26
Autistic Children: New Hope for a Cure (Tinbergen and Tinbergen), 77–78n.
Aversion therapy, 73

Baker, L., 27
Bannochie, M., 5
Barton, S., 27
Behavior
  genetics and, 18
  language and, 48
Behavioral conditioning
  avoiding frightening procedures, 14
  see also Operant conditioning
Behavioral therapy, treatment and, 72–73
Bender, L., 2, 5, 55, 56, 57, 67
Benson, D. F., 52, 53
Bettelheim, B., 1–2, 26, 67–68
  therapy, 67–68
Biological approach, 2, 18–24
  continuity *vs.* discontinuity in personality, 21–24
  genetics and behavior, 18
  holism, 17, 78n.
  individual differences, 18–21
  treatment and, 71–72
  see also Genetics
Blank, M., 46
Blind children, compared with deaf children, 38
Borelli, M., 38
Bowlby, J., 18
Bradshaw, J. L., 54

93

The Author

Cheryl D. Seifert trained in pediatric psychology at The University of Chicago, Wyler Children's Hospital, Department of Pediatrics, Pediatric Mental Development Clinic, Joseph P. Kennedy, Jr., Mental Retardation Center, and specialized in mental development and retardation. She held staff positions at The University of Chicago, Wyler Children's Hospital, Department of Pediatrics, Pediatric Psychological Services; Michael Reese Hospital and Medical Center, Dysfunctioning Child Center; and Mount Sinai Hospital Medical Center of Chicago, Department of Pediatrics, Pediatric Ecology Program.

She is the author of *Case Studies in Autism: A Young Child and Two Adolescents* and *Holistic Interpretation of Autism: A Theoretical Framework.*